They want something productive and substantial in their pleasures; they want to mix actual fruition with their joy.

Alexis de Tocqueville, 1835

TRACK AND ROAD: THE AMERICAN TROTTING HORSE

A VISUAL RECORD 1820 TO 1900 from the

Harry T. Peters *America on Stone* Lithography Collection

BY PETER C. WELSH

Smithsonian Institution Press

Washington, D.C. 1967

© 1967 Smithsonian Institution   Smithsonian Publication 4714   Library of Congress Catalog Card Number: 67–29351   Designed by Crimilda Pontes

To Janie and Peter

CONTENTS

America on Stone   1

The Trotter and the Road   7

The Trotting Turf   43

Trotters under Saddle   61

Trotters in Harness   77

Trotters to Wagon   105

Portraits of Trotters   121

Handbills and Broadsides   145

Trotting Prints in the Peters Collection   153

Printmakers: Names and Addresses   161

Selected References   167

Index   171

ACKNOWLEDGMENTS

I am indebted to the late Harry T. Peters and the catholicity of his collecting and to the Peters family for their generosity in giving his America on Stone Collection to the Smithsonian Institution. I am equally in the debt of Professor Anthony N. B. Garvan of the University of Pennsylvania for a point of view and for an approach to the study and interpretation of cultural materials. My thanks, too, to Professor Norman Holmes Pearson of Yale University, who, in the course of a busy schedule, found time to read and comment on my manuscript. My Smithsonian colleagues Mr. Roger Pineau and Mr. Edgar Howell were also helpful and generous readers of the manuscript in its earliest stages. My immediate associates of the last several years—Mrs. Doris Esch Borthwick, Mrs. Anne Castrodale Golovin, and Mr. Robert Macdonald—were patient and conscientious helpers. The Prints and Photographs Division of the Library of Congress, the Manuscripts Department of the New York Public Library, and the Hall of Fame of the Trotter at Goshen, New York, have all contributed to this study. I am most grateful indeed to Mr. Oliver Jensen, the editor of *American Heritage*, for making available color plates which appeared originally in that magazine. Finally, for the preparation of the manuscript for publication I want to acknowledge the hard work and good humor of Miss Mary Edwards and the staff of the Smithsonian Institution Press.

Peter C. Welsh

"THE SHED"

PUBLISHED BY BREWSTER & CO. OF BROOME ST.

Intensely proud of native accomplishment, Americans in the years following the Revolution consciously emblazoned objects of all kinds with symbols of their political and technical progress. Eagles adorned chests and fine porcelain; steam engines, steamboats, and locomotives enlivened the design of everything from fabrics to bank notes; and frequently, if they could be afforded, portraits of notables and of one's family, as well as engravings of great events, brightened walls in many houses. But generally the visual image, regardless of the kind, was dear. It was, in fact, only shortly before the Victorian era opened that Americans began to enjoy the lithograph, a popular medium that reflected their strong sense of national purpose and gratified their romantic and sentimental aspirations.

In 1818 Bass Otis, a Philadelphia artist, made the first American lithograph by following a technique perfected in Bavaria at the close of the eighteenth century by Alois Senefelder. By 1840 lithography—the reproduction of impressions drawn with a greasy crayon on specially prepared stones—had become a common practice in all the large cities of the United States. In his *America on Stone* Harry T. Peters has documented scores of lithographers and publishers who worked from Boston to New Orleans, from Connecticut to California. The Endicotts (1830–91), the Kelloggs (1833–67), and Sarony, Major and Knapp (1843–71) of New York; Peter Duval (1835–93) and Thomas Sinclair (1839–89) of Philadelphia; and John Bufford (1835–71) and Haskell & Allen (1871–75) of Boston, to name but a few, all produced prints in great variety and thus competed directly with Currier & Ives. Others tended to be more specialized. For example, Henry R. Robinson, who began work at New York in 1833 and continued there until 1851, concentrated for the most part on caricatures and political prints, while Britton and Rey of New York and San Francisco almost exclusively depicted California during the Gold Rush era. Regardless of their specialties, however, few lithographers and print publishers prospered. In contrast to those mentioned above, most ventures in the lithographing business were

short-lived; as a result, printmakers moved from city to city, from east to west, briefly plying their craft and satisfying public demand for a host of lithographic material that ranged from phrenological charts and patent drawings to pew plans for churches and portraits of popular trotting horses.

Unlike the slow tedium of woodcut and copper-plate engraving, the lithographer's stone proved a fast and inexpensive way to mass-produce impressions. For the first time the graphic artist enjoyed a popular market. Prints in infinite variety were sold by the thousands to a public eager to be reminded of the exploits of their heroes, political, military, and sporting, and of the natural grandeur of their country. The lithograph at once found a ready hanging space on office walls and in comfortable parlors. Never before had pictures been so easily produced or so widely distributed, and never had there been such an appropriate art form to cater to the popular taste. Before the great age of lithography ended late in the 1880s, the printmakers had become collectively what Currier & Ives, the most successful practitioners of the art, had long claimed to be, namely, publishers of "Colored Engravings for the People."

Today collectors treasure the bright and garish lithographs, museums and libraries house important collections of them, and Americans increasingly view them with a decided nostalgia. To the social historian, however, the lithograph is more than a graphic technique developed in the nineteenth century or a colorful expression of the popular romanticism of that century. From the lithograph he can gain not only a reasonable approximation of aspects of Victorian life, but, more than that, he can gain an accurate conception of the American Victorian self-image. Though the details of dress be obscure, the way in which it was worn and the purpose of its design are accurately caught by the lithographer. Though battle scenes may seem faulty to the modern military historian, the lithograph shows the way they were visualized and idealized by the civilian and, indeed, by many soldiers of the Civil War. The handles of the hand tools may disturb the modern collector, but the print catches and preserves the respect in which mechanical innovation was held by the general public. Moreover, the very survival of prints gives a kind of index to their historical importance. The more common the print, the surer its evidence of Victorian taste, values, and attitudes.

It was precisely in this connotation that the late Harry T. Peters valued the lithograph and understood its variety, quality, and, above all, its meaning:

Some are crude, it is true, but more are the work of accomplished and talented artists. Some are merely quaint, some mawkishly sentimental and moralistic, and in some melodrama passes for drama. But more have distinction of line and composition, gracious coloring, and conscientious attention to accuracy of detail. All are homely in the best sense; simple, sincere representations of an era that is past. They belong to the genus Americanus and embody so genuine a record of our development and culture that the permanence of their place is assured.

To Harry Peters the lithograph was in reality "America on Stone," a graphic parade touching all phases of American life, and perhaps none appealed to him more than those depicting scenes of the track and road.

Views of well-ordered towns and graceful buildings, great deeds of a young nation, portraits of the prominent, colorful locomotives and steamboats, majestic clippers, dashing sportsmen, sleek thoroughbreds, and sturdy trotters were standard subjects in the lithographic repertory. The romantic and the genre comprise only a fraction of the lithographic material produced, but together with a profusion of political caricatures, temperance reminders, patriotics, religious prints, and commercial advertisements, they captured a burgeoning people enthusiastically responding to the headiness of a democratic faith and the legacy of Poor Richard.

Mr. Peters collected examples of the work of American printmakers with just such an enthusiastic, albeit romantic, view of American society, and his published accounts of their prolific output—*Currier and Ives; Printmakers to the American People* (2 vols.

1929–1931), *America on Stone; the Other Printmakers to the American People* (1931), and *California on Stone* (1935)—remain scarce but standard references. After Mr. Peters' death in 1948 his family separated his collection into three major parts each representing one of his published works. The Currier and Ives Collection was given to the Museum of the City of New York; the California on Stone Collection went to the M. H. de Young Museum, San Francisco, for permanent loan to the San Francisco Historical Society; and lastly, the America on Stone Collection of some 1700 prints by lithographers other than Currier and Ives was presented to the Smithsonian Institution in 1960.

In the chapters that follow, one group of the America on Stone Collection—those depicting the trotting horse on track and road—will be discussed as documents which suggest an important facet of our cultural and historical experience, the quest for recreation. The prints in this group represent a fair random sampling of the total output of such scenes by American lithographers. They do not, however, include all examples published, nor is every champion who trotted to fame and fortune in the nineteenth century to be found among the Peters prints. What is preserved in these prints is a visual record encompassing roughly eighty years of the nineteenth century. It is a parade of people, places, and track performers which, when placed in context by a variety of written records, tends to brighten materially the deeper shades of brown that seem to dominate the Victorian decades.*

* An earlier version of this chapter appeared in Anthony N. B. Garvan and Peter C. Welsh, *The Victorian American* (Washington, D. C., 1961), pp. 9–14.

Paint⁴ by E. Clarkson, Philad⁴.

Lith by A. Hoen & Co. Balto.

ANDREW JACKSON JR.
OWNED BY ARTHUR H. MANN,
BALTIMORE.

WATERING PLACE ON THE ROAD.

Early in the 1850s most authorities who wrote of horses and horsemen surveyed the country's equestrian scene and observed that the breeding, training, and racing of trotting horses was "the people's sport, the people's pastime and, consequently, is, and will be supported by the people." It is little wonder that the lithograph—already the medium of popular art—should reflect in depth the nation's favorite popular pursuit. Harry T. Peters estimated that horse portraits, track scenes, and views of the road were outnumbered only by town views among subjects in the commercial lithographers' repertoire. "Every tradesman, artisan, businessman, or mechanic, whose affairs require the services of a horse, in America, keeps, as that by which he can alone combine profit with pleasure, a fast and hardy trotter"; to all of these the lithographs of famous trotters were an inspiration and a source of emulation.[1] The wedding of the lithograph and the trotting horse was a union of popular taste.

The farmer and the country gentlemen were as devoted to the trotting horse as were their urban counterparts. In city and country alike, "speed, which was formerly little required," was now thought to be "an indispensable requisite in a good horse."[2] Henry William Herbert, better known under the pseudonym Frank Forester, had come to New York from England in 1831 and, until his death in 1858, penned a succession of sports articles and novels describing the excitement of the turf and the joys of field and stream. By the 1830s he estimated that "north and east of the Mason and Dixon's line," in a day's time in any rural district "one will meet, beyond a doubt, a hundred persons travelling in light wagons, sulkies, or chaises, for five—I hardly think I should err, if I were to say for one—on horseback."[3] By midcentury, speed and the saving of time had become a

1. Henry William Herbert [Frank Forester], *Frank Forester's Horse and Horsemanship of the United States and the British Provinces of North America* (New York, 1871), vol. 2, pp. 126–127. Hereafter cited *Frank Forester*. 2. *Eighty Years' Progress of the United States* (Hartford, 1867), vol. 1, p. 52.   3. *Frank Forester*, vol. 2, p. 72.

mania in American life. The advent of steam transportation—land and water—had reduced travel time most spectacularly, but coincident with it was the improvement of the older and more familiar forms of conveyance "manifest in the number and quality of private carriages of all kinds that are now kept by almost all who live out of cities, and by many of those who reside in them."[4] Throughout the country, roads had been improved and remained dry for a longer period each year. The public road had become relatively safe for truly speedy horses; at the same time wagons and harness had attained a real excellence of design, exemplified by the light trotting wagons made by W. D. Rogers & Company of Philadelphia or by Brewster & Company of New York and by the fine horse furnishings turned out by firms like Miller, Morrison & Company. These factors, plus the ubiquitous sporting print, tended to spur pleasure drivers to greater speed.

Contemporary authors credited the railroads for nearly every aspect of American success, even citing them as the stimulus for the general interest in fast horses, "since the greater breadth of land by their means laid open to market" had increased wealth, making it profitable for "all to keep pleasure-vehicles, when formerly the saddle only was used outside the stage-coach."[5] Frank Forester more correctly sensed the "utilitarian maxim of the age that time is money" and saw, as others did with fast ships or locomotives, that "fast horses really are true, hard money."[6] The new delight for speed caused the pleasure, or spring wagon to appear in many a carriage house long "before the piano supplanted the quilting frame in the parlor."[7]

The fast and stylish driver required a "business-wagon of tasteful appearance"; one with "case hardened iron axles, steel springs, and a top buggy." In addition, many persons kept "a rockaway, or even a coach."[8] The horses suitable for such a driver and equipage

4. *Eighty Years' Progress*, vol. 1, p. 360.   5. Ibid.   6. *Frank Forester*, vol. 1, pp. 484–485.   7. *Eighty Years' Progress*, vol. 1, p. 360.   8. Ibid.

were known as roadsters, and they were in a great demand. "Pleasure-driving," wrote an enthusiast in 1857, "has become a national amusement," a pastime "for which a growing passion is to be noticed among all classes of our citizens." Newfound leisure time among "our tradesmen and mechanics" enabled them in increasing numbers

*to indulge in sports and amusements involving but a moderate expense, such for instance as the
keeping of a birddog and gun, for a few days recreation in the summer, and in the luxury of a fine
driving horse, with which they give their wives and children an occasional airing. The importance
of this particularly American amusement can hardly be overestimated; it affords a mode of recreation both for the mind and body, of the most pleasant and useful kind.[9]*

And it was precisely the popularity of this "mode of recreation" that prompted Currier &
Ives to publish "Out for a days Shooting," a print which featured a pair of dapper hunts-
men flying along in a road wagon behind a pair of fast-stepping trotters.

 Brief and pleasurable outings taken at a swift pace were but one test of a good roadster.
Sustained performance was a trait no less highly prized than speed, and it was an attribute
frequently attested. It was the consensus in the nineteenth century that every horse bred
in the United States was in some sense suited for the road. Most commentators agreed that
"for docility, temper, soundness of constitution, endurance of fatigue, hardness, sure-
footedness and speed, the American roadster is not to be excelled, if equalled, by any horse
in the known world not purely thoroughbred."[10] The stamina of the American trotter,
when properly utilized, seemed boundless, and the fitness demanded of a driver frequently
approached that of his horses.

*On one occasion, [wrote Frank Forester] in the extremely hot summer of 1838, I drove a pair of
horses, before a sporting wagon, which loaded, with myself, my friend, my servant and a brace
of setters included, weighed something over seventeen hundred weight, from the city of New*

9. D. C. Linsley, *Morgan Horses* (New York, 1857), pp. 50–51. 10. *Frank Forester*, vol. 1, p. 112.

York, to Niagara Falls and back, including excursions to shoot, and deviations from the route. We were forty-one days on the road. . . .[11]

The roadster was an accepted institution in American life from the 1820s forward, and one that existed in considerable variety. Lithographers conveyed this variety even in their most stereotyped renditions of the road, as did the writers of the period when they attempted to explain why one particular type or color of horse appealed to one person rather than another. Moreover, in horseflesh—as in most aspects of nineteenth-century American society—regional differences could be strong. Not infrequently, the type of horse found in newly settled areas was as sure an indication of cultural transfer as was the architectural style and construction of a dwelling.

The traveler in the middle decades of the nineteenth century found New England's horses to be of medium size, compactly formed, hardy, gentle, and particularly tractable as driving horses. In the New England countryside one could find nearly everywhere the descendants of Justin Morgan, and in parts of Massachusetts and Connecticut the influence of French Canada could be traced by the prevalence of Norman, Flemish, and Danish horses. The English racers and Arabians also left their marks in the northern states; the common horse stock of rural New England was infused with the blood of Imported Messenger, the Dey of Algiers, Post Boy, Sir Walter, and Sir Charles, notables among imported stallions.[12]

In New York State the variety of horses was even greater than in New England. The driving horses, "many of them very fine," were taller and less compact. The average farm and draft horses were also more robust than those of New England. Although the thoroughbred was more prevalent in the early part of the century, by the 1850s the standardbred was the fashion, for the descendants of Imported Messenger, Eclipse, Henry, and

11. Ibid., vol. 2, p. 484.   12. Linsley, *Morgan Horses*, p. 24.

Duroc had given New York horse breeders a foundation that rapidly produced some of the finest trotters and studs ever sired. In central and northern New York the Morgans began to be seen after the middle of the century. Nevertheless, the reputation of New York horses rested upon Hambletonian, the unquestioned king of trotting-horse progenitors and a favorite of the horse portraitists.

Farms of New Jersey and eastern Pennsylvania, like those of New York, were stocked with excellent roadsters of every pedigree. On westward, however, a traveler with a good eye might notice considerable change in the characteristics of horses. Fine driving horses were more rare, and the farm and draft animals were often immense, particularly in areas of German settlement and in southern Ohio. In clear contrast was the northern part of that state, the Western Reserve, where the New England influence could be seen in the number and variety of good roadsters and fancy wagons. Farther to the west and northwest the horses tended to resemble those of northern Ohio. In Kentucky and Tennessee fine saddle horses and a nucleus of carefully bred trotters and runners were to be found, many of whom traced their antecedents to New York.

Finally, in the deep South the trotter enjoyed little or no popularity at all. Here the mule was used as a draft animal on both farm and road. The English thoroughbred (or his derivative) persisted as the planter's mount for both the race course and the hunt. "Light wagons," wrote Linsley, were "but little used." The population was scattered, and, although carriages were maintained by southern families, travel was "principally upon horseback." It was no myth that in the South horsemen preferred a "handsome well-broken and well-bitted galloper."[13]

Whatever his geography, however, in the selection of a roadster even the most style-conscious had a wide latitude of choice. Any of a number of good trotting "families" had

13. Ibid., pp. 25–27; *Frank Forester*, vol. 1, p. 115.

been fathered by such stalwarts as Justin Morgan, Black Hawk, Hambletonian, and Mambrino Chief. In choosing a horse there was also, of course, a high degree of personal taste involved. One buyer wanted a horse that was "round and smooth, with soft hair, a beautiful color, and a proud, showy style"—one not too fast or with any great endurance, an animal that would "attract the admiration of his neighbors." Another was concerned only with acquiring a horse "on account of his useful qualities." In addition, color was a serious criterion to many horse owners. "White, light grey, light sorrel, cream-colored, and spotted" were objectionable, while bays, chestnuts, blacks, and dark browns were considered *de rigueur* and were "worth more in every market." This fact notwithstanding, printmakers included in their views of the road ample numbers of whites, spotted, and creams, which contrasted nicely with the neatly and artistically arranged blacks and bays. Individuals might differ in their preferences for color, for the style of movement of their buggy horses, and, indeed, for the type of buggy that they should drive, "yet the anxiety to own a free, nimble driver" was a trait that "might almost be styled a national characteristic."[14]

Foreign visitors who wrote of their travels in the United States, as well as those who commented on our various levels of technological progress, provided some vivid and detailed statements about our horses and buggies and about our uses for them. The American buggy or sulky was a favorite topic. There are few better descriptions than that by the Britisher, James W. Burgess, who in 1881 wrote a historical and descriptive account of coach building. Many a lithograph, colorful and inaccurate in detail, still suggests, as Burgess explained, that

the Americans have lavished all their ingenuity upon these buggies, and they have arrived at a marvelous perfection of lightness. They are hung upon two elliptical springs. The axles and car-

14. Linsley, *Morgan Horses*, pp. 250–251, 258.

GOING TO THE TROT.

riage timber have been reduced to mere thin sticks. The four wheels are made so slender as to resemble a spider's web. Instead of the circumference of the wheel being composed of a number of felloes, they consist of only two of oak or hickory wood, bent to shape by steam. The ironwork is very slender and yet composed of many pieces, and in order to reduce the cost these pieces are mostly cast, not forged, of a sort of iron less brittle than our cast-iron. The bodies are of light work like what we call cabinet work. The weight of the whole vehicle is so small that one man can easily lift it upon its wheels again if it should be incidentally upset, and two persons of ordinary strength can raise it easily from the ground.[15]

In the horse and road prints in the Peters Collection the folios advertising Brewster & Company of New York—one by Sarony, Major, and Knapp, and one by Endicott & Company—are of a quality commensurate with the wagons and the firm they recommended. The lithograph by A. Hoen & Co. of Baltimore after a painting by Clarkson is a particularly good rendering of the fine wagons that so appealed to the Englishman Burgess.

The commentary of travelers, foreign and domestic, correlates well with the printmakers' view of the road. Boston's Brighton Road, where the boys were "wont to exercise their fast nags,"[16] and New York's Harlem Lane, which enjoyed "a wide reputation with the lovers of the turf,"[17] were most frequently pictured and perhaps best known. Then, too, there was Philadelphia's Rope Ferry Road, the popular thoroughfare to Point Breeze Park and the races. Scenes in the big cities, particularly in the East, were a reflection in greater scale of the drivers, horses, and wagons pounding stylishly along in towns and hamlets throughout the country. In August of 1861 that opinionated Britisher, Anthony Trollope, was visiting Newport, Rhode Island. He had found American saddle horses so generally lacking in éclat that he was led to comment on the "general smartness" and number of

15. James W. Burgess, *A Practical Treatise on Coach-Building Historical and Descriptive* (London, 1881), pp. 146–148.   16. *Chandler's Visitor's Guide in and around Boston* (Boston, 1870), p. 91.   17. Junius Henry Browne, *The Great Metropolis; A Mirror of New York* (Hartford, 1869), p. 571.

POINT
VIEW
E. STURCE.

New York, Publ by Th: Kelly, 35 Bowery.

TROTTING CRACKS ON THE ROAD
SCENE — HARLEM LANE

carriages that he saw. "It seemed" to Trollope "that every lady with a horse of her own had also her own carriage." In Newport—and for that matter everywhere else—the "carriages were always open." It was almost "the law of land," one that fashion demanded, that the occupants of these rigs have their knees covered "with a worked worsted apron of brilliant colours." At first impression Trollope thought that these lap robes "seemed tawdry; but the eye soon becomes used to bright colours, in carriage aprons as well as in architecture." Trollope quickly learned to like them.[18]

Although printmakers frequently ignored the technical details of harness or carriage appurtenances, they seldom missed the latest styles. The road prints documented most colorfully the preference of the day for the bright blues, reds, and golds that drivers sported in their choice of carriage robes. Notable in this respect are the prints by Kelly of New York and by Haskell & Allen of Boston.

John Henry Vessey, an English tourist less outspoken than Trollope, in 1859 noted that buffalo hides and even white bearskins were used as carriage robes. Few persons either had or kept a liveried coachman, but when on occasion Vessey saw one he was usually "a black man." Vessey observed that London horses were sleeker and glossier in appearance than those of American cities, owing largely, he thought, to milder winters. But if he was a bit critical of the groomed appearance of the horses he was enthusiastic about American carriages and the fine traits of the horses that pulled them. That they were "peculiarly light and easy to run" was Vessey's first impression of American carriages. "The wheels must be made of the best material to stand the wear and tear of the streets." The spokes of these vehicles were only one third "the thickness of those in English carriages," and the "light buggy wagon," without top, weighed only 175 to 220 pounds. He marveled at the training of the buggy horses; apparently in his travels he had seen few restive animals. Like Trol-

18. Anthony Trollope, *North America* (New York, 1862), pp. 25–26.

lope, Vessey noted that "riding is not the fashionable amusement with the American people, they seem to delight in driving these fast trotting horses in the light buggies." Predictably, Vessey, as an Englishman, was interested in the American style of horse racing. He found it to be mostly trotting and noted that the best time for the mile had been steadily reduced from about 2:40 to 2:24½.[19]

In 1870 the professional travel writer and commentator George Makepeace Towle supported Vessey's earlier view when in his more detailed account of American society he wrote that "racing, yachting, and kindred sports grow more popular every year. Especially in New York are horses the rage."[20] Those who knew New York well, like the popular journalist of the *Tribune,* Junius Henri Browne, concurred with Towle. Nothing, wrote Browne, had developed more rapidly in the great Metropolis than "the quality of its horses. The last ten or twelve years have made a revolution in horse-flesh. Men now drive, and have an enthusiasm about blooded stock, who, until recently, had no interest in the turf, or anything belonging to it. They were satisfied to jog along behind slow and somber steeds." But no longer was this the case. According to this chronicler of the city, New Yorkers, and in fact most Americans, had caught "the fetlock fever."[21] The intensity and degree to which the fever ran is well measured by the number of surviving track and road prints published in the last half of the century with Currier & Ives alone responsible for over five hundred separate titles.

Trotting horses were purchased by men of affluence as marks of status and were driven for pleasure. The practice—for those who could afford it—was to purchase the brightest stars from the trotting track. The market for good horseflesh thus created made every man a driver and every thoroughfare a likely spot for a test of speed. In 1871 it was the opinion

19. *Mr. Vessey of England. Being the Incidents and Reminiscences of Travel in a Twelve Weeks' Tour through the United States and Canada in the Year 1859,* edit. Brian Waters (New York, 1956), pp. 36–37. 20. George Makepeace Towle, *American Society* (London, 1870), vol. 2, p. 27. 21. Browne, *Great Metropolis,* p. 558.

of John Elderken, a widely published writer on the subject of horses and horsemen, that "the racecourse in America is in fact gradually becoming merely an exercising ground for the development and training of horses previous to their passage into the hands of gentlemen who could keep them solely for their own amusement."[22] The road prints in the Peters Collection support Elderken's opinion. The height of so-called fashionable driving is captured in the print "Taking the Reins." It shows the trotting horse Dexter driven by none other than General Grant, while Dexter's owner, Robert Bonner, publisher of the *New York Ledger,* sits stiffly and properly beside him. Thomas Kelly's print of 1870, "Watering Place on the Road," depicts a scene only slightly less fashionable than that of "Taking the Reins." The print shows John Barry's roadhouse, and, in front of it in their rigs, such notables of the day as Foster Dewey, Robert Bonner, Timothy Eastman, and A. J. Gillander. Another lively print, "Trotting Cracks of Philadelphia Returning from the Race in Point Breeze Park," was also published in 1870, and, like the majority of prints in this group, it portrays the leading gentlemen-horsemen of the day. This time, however, top billing is given, not to the drivers, but to their horses: Fanny Allen, Bay Mary, Ironsides and mate, Harry D., Black Maggie, Lady Lightfoot, Sunbeam, Young Trafalgar, Victor Patchen, Bay George, Mack, Red Cloud, Victoria, Sun Flower, General Birney and mate, Moscow, Joe Parker Pony, and, finally, Napoleon. Robert Bonner's team of Dexter and Goldsmith Maid and William Vanderbilt's Mountain Boy are the subject of "Fast Horses of New York" published in 1871 by Thomas Kelly. Such a print presumably encouraged trotting buffs to new heights in emulating the best horseflesh on any road.

Two prints by Haskell & Allen of Boston round out the summer road scenes in the Peters Collection. The first is entitled "Leaving Brighton Hotel for the Mill-Dam," and the

22. John Elderken, "Turf and Trotting Horse of America," *Every Horse Owners' Cyclopedia,* edit. Robert McClure (Philadelphia, 1872), p. 553. The price of the best trotting stock had increased about 100 percent every decade after 1830.

"TAKING THE REINS"

DRAWN BY JOHN W. EHNINGER.

THE CELEBRATED TROTTING-HORSE DEXTER DRIVEN BY GENERAL GRANT

AND ROBERT BONNER ESQ. OWNER OF DEXTER AND PROPRIETOR OF THE N.Y. LEDGER.

[20]

TROTTING CRACKS OF PHILADELPHIA RETURNING FROM THE RACE AT POINT BREEZE PARK,

HAVING A BRUSH PAST TURNER'S HOTEL, ROPE FERRY ROAD, PHILADELPHIA, 1870.

Respectfully Dedicated to the Lovers of Horses and the Sporting Public in general by the Publisher.

PUBLISHED BY H. PHARAZYN, 1738 LOMBARD STREET.   ENTERED ACCORDING TO ACT OF CONGRESS, IN THE YEAR 1870, IN THE DISTRICT COURT OF THE UNITED STATES FOR THE EASTERN DISTRICT OF PENNSYLVANIA.

New York. Pub'd by "C" Kelly.

BONNERS, DEXTER & GOLDSMITH MAID   VANDERBILTS, MOUNTAIN BOY   From an Original Sketch by J. Beard.

FAST HORSES, OF N.Y.   SCENE HARLEM LANE N.Y.

TROTTING CRACKS ON THE BRIGHTON ROAD.
(SCENE, MILE GROUND.)

other, "Trotting Cracks on the Brighton Road." Justin Winsor in his *Memorial History of Boston* cited the particular appeal in the early 1880s of the Brighton Road, where there was always "constant pleasure travel from Boston proper."[23] It was, however, at the mill dam—on Brighton Road—that the trotting and spirited driving were done, and there in winter the sleighs raced. As *Bacon's Dictionary of Boston* pointed out on "early summer or late autumn afternoons" the road was "brilliant with handsome teams and gay turnouts presenting an exhilarating spectacle worth taking a good deal of trouble to see."[24]

The road was not always subject to the caprices of the weather. Frances Trollope in the early 1830s found nothing so agreeable as sleighing. Hiram Woodruff also wrote nostalgically of the 1840s and of the "sleigh-riding, when the air is keen and frosty, the sky clear, the snow deep and crisp." By 1868 in New York City, however, along some of the old favorite routes the sound of bells and the crunch of snow under a trotter's hoofs had largely disappeared. "The street railroads," wrote Woodruff, "have done for all that."[25] Nonetheless, in country towns and villages the road in winter remained the delight so often seen in the lithographic views published by the New England lithographers Bufford and Haskell & Allen or preserved in the spirited description of the travel writer George Makepeace Towle, experiencing and enumerating the joys of an American winter.

Then the sleighing! On some cold November morning you wake up to hear, in every direction, hundreds of liquid tinkling bells. You glance out of your bedroom window; the earth is clothed, the houses are mantled with a heavy feathery crust of snow, and hither and thither are jingling the sleighs, the whips are lustily cracking, the horses themselves feel the infection in the air, and run briskly, jumping and bounding as if they too rejoiced that the snow had come. Sleighs of every

23. Justin Winsor, *The Memorial History of Boston* (Boston, 1880), vol. 3, p. 610.   24. George E. Ellis, *Bacon's Dictionary of Boston* (Boston, 1886), p. 71.   25. See Frances Trollope, *Domestic Manners of the Americans*, edit. Donald Smalley (New York, 1949), p. 304, and Hiram Woodruff, *The Trotting Horse of America* (New York, 1868), p. 186.

ENTERED ACCORDING TO ACT OF CONGRESS, IN THE YEAR 1871, BY HASKELL & ALLEN, IN THE OFFICE OF THE LIBRARIAN OF CONGRESS AT WASHINGTON.
PUBLISHED BY HASKELL & ALLEN, 14 HANOVER STREET, BOSTON.

LEAVING BRIGHTON HOTEL FOR THE MILL-DAM
SUMMER

ENTERED ACCORDING TO ACT OF CONGRESS, IN THE YEAR 1875, BY MASKELL & ALLEN, IN THE OFFICE OF THE LIBRARIAN OF CONGRESS AT WASHINGTON.
PUBLISHED BY MASKELL & ALLEN, 14 HANOVER STREET, BOSTON.

LEAVING BRIGHTON HOTEL FOR THE MILL-DAM
WINTER

sort and size; shell-shaped sleighs, lavishly adorned, brass-rimmed; heavy square sleighs, full of buffalo robes and wrappers; sleighs which are but carts on runners, in one of which your milk man dashes up, and from which he brings out his long tin can; basket sleighs—modest affairs—adopted on a sudden, because the snow was not so soon expected; and great excursion sleighs, with gaudy paint and quaint figureheads; some triumphal cars, after the Roman model, others looking like circus vans, wherein ere long, you will see troops of children on their way to the suburbs for a glowing ride, and merry youthful parties bound for a hearty frolic.[26]

It is conceivable that Towle had never experienced an American winter but had only the lithographic views to stimulate his imagination. "A Home in the Country," published by Thomas Kelly of New York, or "The Farmers Home," published by Charles Brothers and drawn by Charles Hart, more than suggest the scenes that Towle described, and even more emphatically than did Towle they illustrate those strengths of the Victorian century: family, home, and church. The graceful Albany cutters illustrated in John Kelly's version of a "Winter Scene in the Country" contrast the two-horse, four-place type and the stylish two-seater pulled by a single, sprightly, fast-stepping trotter. And again by contrast, in Haskell & Allen's "Winter" the viewer sees a heavy-duty, ox-drawn work sled, children belly-flopping on their wooden runners and—surpassing all in terms of status, pleasure, and dash—a four-seater rounding a curve at a brisk clip with that sportiest of all winter companions in the lead, the American trotting horse. If there are any doubts about the expansiveness of the Yankee character on snow-packed roads, they are quickly dispelled by reference to prints such as Kimmel & Forster's "Winter Pleasure in the Country" and midwestern pieces like Hughes & Johnson's "A Merry Christmas, A Happy New-Year" published as an advertisement for Putnum's Clothing House at Clark and Madison Streets in Chicago.

26. Towle, *American Society*, vol. 2, p. 30.   27. Marjorie D. Ross, *Book of Boston* (New York, 1901), p. 29.

A Home in the Country

WINTER

PUBLISHED BY THOMAS KELLY 17 BARCLAY ST N Y

WINTER IN THE COUNTRY.- THE FARMERS HOME.

WINTER SCENE in the COUNTRY.

PRINTED BY Wm H. REESE 195 CHAM ST N.Y.

PUBLISHED BY KELLOGG & CO., HARTFORD, PHILADELPHIA & JAMES REESE 196 N.Y.

BOSTON. PUBLISHED & LITH BY J.H.BUFFORD, 313 WASHN ST.

WINTER.

GOING TO A CHRISTMAS PARTY.

Published by Chr. Kimmel & Forster 254 & 256 Canal St. N.Y.

WINTER PLEASURE IN THE COUNTRY.

WINTER.

FEARNAUGHT STALLIONS,

OWNED BY DAVID NEVINS Jr, FRAMINGHAM, MASS.

From the Original Painti.. by ...

FEARNAUGHT BOY BY THE OLD HORSE - LANCET .. MICH.

Untitled. "J. Cameron."

The winter views depicting sleighing courses differ little in subject matter and in spirit, quality, and tone from the summer road scenes. Fashionable men, their ladies wrapped in furs and covered with heavy blankets, are seen dashing madly (and with less order than in summer) along packed-down roads, some racing, some proceeding leisurely, some alone, some with family—but none on wheels. Marjorie D. Ross in her *Book of Boston* wrote in 1901 that "sleighing out Beacon Street and over Mill-Dam to the Brighton Road was a favorite sport."[27] In 1906 *The Boston Herald* reported that "All Boston Spent the Sabbath on Runners, and Parkways and Country Roads Heard Sleigh Bells Symphony."[28] Bufford's lithograph entitled "Winter/Going to a Christmas Party" conveys the spirit typical of the press reports that filled Boston newspapers in the wintertime. If there is any doubt that racing on hard-packed snow was full of excitement, simply look at the prints published in 1875 by Haskell & Allen of the "Fearnaught Stallions" and their owner, David Nevins, Jr., of Framingham, Massachusetts. These two prints commemorate not only the superb stallions but also the sleek and graceful lines of the Albany cutter. The final print among the winter road scenes is an untitled colored lithograph signed by J. Cameron, the artist who worked so long for Currier & Ives; the excitement of the sleigh race which this print depicts is as fresh today as when Cameron drew it. The joviality of just such an American winter scene, with dashing sleds and sleighs, skaters and people, from house to house "taking their hot toddy to keep the cold out,"[29] had convinced Towle that "when you see an American sleighing-course, you will perhaps judge [New Englanders] . . . a less tristful and sombre people than you had thought."[30]

The road brought, along with its pleasures, a share of humor to American life. Palmer's satirical print of the "B'hoys," Jones and Newman's fun-poking at the etiquette of the road,

28. *The Boston Herald*, February 12, 1906.   29. Woodruff, *Trotting Horse*, p. 186.   30. Towle, *American Society*, vol. 2, p. 32.

and M. J. Warner's several views of the "One Hoss Shay," all, in one way or another, made use of Holmes' image of the "rat-tailed, ewe-necked bay" that pulled the "Deacon's Masterpiece." These comic prints lampooned and deflated the questionable virtues of Yankee brag and American superiority. Writers, too, piqued the overexuberance of national pride. In 1871 Thomas Chandler Haliburton chose the trotting horse as a symbol of this in the first chapter of *The Clockmaker*. The dialogue between Sam Slick of Slickville and his companion permitted most Americans to hear themselves:

"I never part with a horse, sir, that suits me," said he. "I am fond of a horse: I don't like to ride in the dust after every one I meet, and I allow no man to pass me but when I choose."[31]

Edward Noyes Westcott, through his character David Harum, also conveyed in a humorous way some of the simple truths and sage advice so often delineated by the printmakers. The relative position of the horse in the value scale of upstate New York residents in the last quarter of the nineteenth century is delightfully pinpointed when David sums up Deakin Perkins' strengths: "Next to the deakin's religious experience, them of lawin' an' horse-tradin' air his strongest p'ints, an' he works the hull on 'em to once sometimes." Or again as David, looking better by comparison, modestly admits: "I'm quite a liar myself when it comes right down to the hoss bus'nis, but the deakin e'n give me both bowers ev'ry hand." The usual and expected probity of business vanished in horse dealings: "A hoss trade ain't like anythin' else. A feller may be straighter'n a string in ev'rythin' else, an' never tell the truth—that is, the hull truth—about a hoss." It was man's sense that made the horse, and David Harum could confide: "Hosses don't know but dreadful little, really. Talk about hoss sense—wa'al, the' ain't no sech thing." The incongruities of an age make humor, and the confrontation of Harum's trotter and a road engine (steam plow) "wee-

31. Thomas Chandler Haliburton, *The Clockmaker. Sayings and Doings of Samuel Slick of Slickville* (Boston and New York, 1871), p. 6.

WAKE UP THERE! WHAT'R YE 'BOUT?

Nº 3.

Published by E. Jones, & G. W. Newman, 122 Fulton St Sun Building.

Series Nº 3.

TWO OF THE B'HOYS.

No 4. Breaking.

DEACON JONES' ONE HOSS SHAY. Nº 1.

COPYRIGHT 1879, BY M.J. WARNER.

DEACON JONES' ONE HOSS SHAY. Nº 2.

wawed putty near square across" the road was but a portent of what would befall the trotter as a new century dawned.[32]

Currier & Ives, the best known of the nineteenth-century lithographers, at an early date billed themselves as publishers of "Colored Engravings for the People," a sobriquet applicable to most American printmakers. The yearning to own the fastest trotter and—manners notwithstanding—to lead the pack, the brisk, clipped expression, and the dogmatic certainty of being and owning the best, all were qualities caught by the lithographer. For the printmaker was first and foremost the people's artist, capitalizing upon their attitudes, both popular and unpopular. Like the writer of this period, he saw in the zest for speed, for the joys of the road, and for good horses traits that, in caricature, made his audience laugh at themselves.

32. Edward Noyes Westcott, *David Harum: A Story of American Life* (New York, 1898), pp. 7–8, 171–172, 294.

Attendance at trotting matches rivaled pleasure driving as a popular pastime. Throughout the age of American lithography "private and public trotting matches in harness" were, according to one well-known encyclopedist of the horse, "the chief amusement of the town population." Tracks were everywhere, and county and state agricultural fairs were popular attractions, more because of the caliber of trotting matches they featured than for the prize livestock exhibited. Trotting matches in Victorian America were, "in fact, the national sport."[1] The impact of horse racing, particularly harness racing, between the 1830s and 1870s was captured succinctly in *Frank Leslie's Illustrated Newspaper:* "But to go once to the Fashion Course [Long Island] on a race day is to be sympathetic for the turf and for all the turfy in its varied ramifications."[2]

To this sympathy the printmakers catered, and they frequently knew their market better than they knew the turf. They made available to track enthusiasts a variety of scenes for office walls, livery stables, and roadhouses. These bright and often garish pictures idealized the horse, vividly portrayed the prized virtues of speed and stamina, commemorated famous drivers and trainers, advertised important studs and stud farms, and, most important, sold—and sold well—for a dollar and sometimes for three or more. Lithographers who published prints of the track judged correctly the country's devotion to the trotter and the average American's first taste of mass recreation, leisure, and spectator sport. The trotting prints and the press must be examined together, for throughout most of the nineteenth century—the heyday of harness racing—the two media are inseparable.

Trotting matches of the 1820s were recorded in the newspapers and in the *American Turf Register and Sporting Magazine,* and the *American Farmer* consistently noted harness meets during this period. The Long Island tracks, Centreville and the Union Course, and Philadelphia's Hunting Park attracted modest crowds for trotting events during this

1. Robert McClure, ed., *Every Horse Owners' Cyclopedia* (Philadelphia, 1872), p. 50. 2. "The Opening Day on Fashion Course," *Frank Leslie's Illustrated Newspaper,* vol. 2 (June 28, 1856), p. 44.

decade. Printmakers in the 1820s captioned their work with detailed and dated descriptions of their subjects' best times and records. In addition to the press and a few periodicals, the New York and Long Island Trotting Clubs and Philadelphia's "Hunting Park Association for the Improvement of Trotting Horses" gave impetus to a spectator sport which grew steadily in the 1830s and 1840s. During these years Americans adopted their first popular sport heroes—the trotting horse Lady Suffolk (affectionately called "The Old Gray Mare") and her trainer and driver, the incomparable Hiram Woodruff.

The 1850s brought continued growth. Trotting matches came to dominate agricultural fairs, and nearly year-round meetings from April through November provided a lively interest for all levels of society. New favorites appeared and a succession of popular trotters replaced Lady Suffolk as equine ruler of the day. "Celebrated American Trotting Horses," a lithograph by W. H. Rease, published by Wagner & McGuigan of Philadelphia in 1854, groups the best and most popular of the midcentury trotting stalwarts. From the sixties onward until the end of the century the trotting mania magnified, and a series of prints—whose emphasis was always on speed and on records set—documents in portraits and action scenes a successive wave of champions: Dexter, Ethan Allen, Goldsmith Maid, Flora Temple, Rarus, St. Julien, and Cresceus, to list but a few. While these prints from the Peters Collection do not illustrate all of the record-breaking performances of the century, they come close to doing so.

When Yankee trotted the mile in 1806 in 2:59, the lithograph had not yet been adapted to the demands of a popular art form. When, however, the assault upon the two-minute mile began in earnest between 1840 and 1860, Lady Suffolk's 2:26½ in 1844, Tacony's 2:25½ in 1853, and Flora Temple's best time of 2:19¾ in 1859 were top subjects for this relatively new medium. In the sixties Dexter, in a series of spectacular efforts which led to his finest time of 2:17¼, was most frequently illustrated in company with his arch rival, Ethan Allen. Between 1871 and 1878 came Goldsmith Maid. Her best efforts eventually

lowered the mile mark to 2:14, and then, as the decade closed, Rarus reduced it to 2:13¼.
The printmakers, never missing a bet, published colorful views documenting these achievements. In the 1880s St. Julien's 2:12¾ and Maud S's 2:10+ efforts, together with the final thrust toward the two-minute barrier by Cresceus in the nineties, commanded the attention of the lithographers. By this date, however, the photograph had already infringed upon the printmakers' monopoly on advertising and documenting the famous firsts of the trotting turf.

From the prints publicizing record achievements may be traced the rise of the "driving parks" at Point Breeze, Cambridge, Mystic (Massachusetts), Hartford, Rochester, Cleveland, Saginaw, Chicago, and, in the far West, San Francisco and Oakland. The trotting-horse prints preserved in the several categories of the Peters Collection vividly illustrate the evolution of the sport from local jockey-club sponsorship, through the heyday of the agricultural fair, and finally to the stature of a national pastime operating as a big business and epitomized by the Grand Circuit, the exuberance of the press, and the size of the crowds that flocked to enjoy trotting matches.

Press announcements of trotting-match results were brief in the early nineteenth century, and their steady increase in length and detail is an obvious measure of the sport's growing importance. Philadelphia's *Daily Chronicle* in May 1828 laconically informed its readers that "the purse of $300 and a silver cup, three miles and repeat, which was trotted for on Thursday, in the vicinity of Philadelphia, was won by the New York horse Screwdriver, in two heats. Time—first heat, 8m. 4s.; second heat, 8m. 10s. This is the fastest trotting time we ever heard of."[3]

The National Gazette did little more for its sports-minded readers in reporting on October 19, 1832, that "a trotting match came off yesterday at the Hunting Park Course" with

3. *The Daily Chronicle* (Philadelphia), May 17, 1828.

Columbus winning over Sally Miller and Comet. Press coverage increased, however, as public interest developed in Lady Suffolk's exploits. According to the *New York Daily Tribune*, the Beacon Course at Camden, New Jersey, was "thronged with the gentry of the turf" on July 12, 1843, to see Albert Conklin, a top rider, steer the Old Gray Mare against a good field that included Hiram Woodruff and J. Spicer, two of the best under-saddle competitors of the century.[4] Crowds at trotting matches now ranged regularly upward of five thousand persons.

The thrill and enjoyment of a good heat was not all that was imbibed at races up and down the eastern seaboard. This is evident in the description of a day spent at the Cambridge track, as reported in 1849 by *The Cambridge Chronicle:*

On Thursday last a race came off at the "Course" in this city, which is deserving a passing notice. It was considered a great occasion by those who take pleasure in such amusements; so we should judge, by the immense number of vehicles, some of which were crowded to excess, which passed over the road to the scene of operation. The roads were excessively dusty, from the want of rain, and the racing on them between West Cambridge and Boston, must have been anything but agreeable. One of the horses on the Course beat anything ever before heard of—trotting his mile in two minutes and twenty-six seconds! This was rapid travelling—equal to the locomotives. And here, as we understand it, was an important point settled, and settled forever, viz: that a horse can travel a mile in a very short space of time! Another feat performed, which should also be chronicled as a fact deserving attention, is, that more liquor was drank that afternoon, than was ever drank before, in the same space of time, in this great city. The quantity was about in proportion to the speed of the fastest horse. Now, we have come to the conclusion, that the advantages resulting from horse racing are to be found in the improvement of the breed of horses; and that the benefits accruing from fast drinking will be manifest in the improvement of the other breed!"[5]

The 1850s found mixed emotions in many trotting-horse enthusiasts. Gambling and drinking as moral problems had come under heavy debate. People heard that the agricul-

4. *New York Daily Tribune*, July 13, 1843.   5. *The Cambridge Chronicle*, June 21, 1849.

tural fairs—conceived earlier by Elkanah Watson and others to demonstrate and exhibit improvements in agricultural techniques and animal husbandry—were being corrupted "by the exciting scenes upon the circular track." The *American Agriculturist* appealed to those who wished to preserve the original spirit and intent of such fairs to make their opinions vocal. The editors were convinced that "during the middle of each day, when nine-tenths of the people visit the grounds, their whole attention has been drawn off to 'trials of speed.'" The best areas, the finest accommodations, and the most money were going to the track instead of to the exhibitors. The Bufford print of Sherman Black Hawk at the United States Agricultural Fair in 1856 at Philadelphia, with crowded stands and infield pavillions in its background, gives an insight into the editors' complaint. Nor was their complaint a mere gentle protest. It conveyed clearly that the track and the trotter, not the farmer, were the real concern of the public who visited the fairgrounds. "We have no sympathy with the race course in any shape; we cannot see anything admirable in the spectacle of two or more horses on a track whipped and goaded to the utmost, by human-monkey riders in jockey caps. If others enjoy such sports, let them seek an appropriate time and place. We claim that they have no right to introduce such sports, surreptitiously or otherwise, upon grounds set apart for the exhibition of the products of agricultural skill and industry."[6]

Frank Forester, entrenched on the other side of this question—representing the horseman's and sportsman's viewpoint, thought "the pundits of the Agricultural Societies" were "fanatical," "foolish," and "prick-eared," as in fact was anyone "who would prohibit the exhibition of speed at their fairs." Nevertheless, Forester did condemn the excesses of the track. He lamented the gambler's influence and the slow withdrawal of the "gentry" as controllers of the sport. But protest was to no avail.[7]

6. *American Agriculturist*, vol. 16 (November 1857: new series), p. 247.   7. *Frank Forester*, vol. 2, p. 130.

The question of the agricultural fairground as a proper place for trotting matches and other moral issues lost vitality with the success of such popular and gifted trotting favorites as Dexter, Flora Temple, American Girl, and Goldsmith Maid. These horses, by proving their stamina and speed, captured the public's fancy. Ironically, most of the outstanding performers owed their very existence to the dedication of the agriculturalists and to their quest for an improved American livestock. With this goal at least, the devotees of the track had to agree. By the 1860s and early 1870s—interrupted but little and actually speeded by the Civil War—the trotting track became a popular institution. Its events were national news. Its champions' names were household words. Its manipulation was big business.

Few descriptions convey better the growth, the impact, the implications, or the color of harness racing in this period than the extended account given by *The Boston Daily Globe* of a midweek trot at Mystic Park. It was a test to try the qualities of the stallion Smuggler and one which, after it was completed, prompted the issue of a spirited print by the Boston firm of Haskell & Allen. In the best hyperbole of the press, enough to inspire an artist, the lead ran "OUR DERBY." The story never lost the pace:

The great stallion race of the century, an event looked forward to by the sporting world this side of the water for many months, occurred at Mystic Park, yesterday, and proved the most successful affair ever witnessed in this country. The entries closed at the Revere House some months ago, and when they were opened nominations to the purse were found to have been received, from Massachusetts, six; New York, three; Connecticut, two; and one each from New Hampshire, Rhode Island, Missouri, Michigan, and California, making a total of sixteen entries for the race. . . . The description and result of the race, together with the scenes incidental, are related below, the race being won by the now famous stallion Smuggler, belonging to Colonel Russell of the Home Farm, Milton, Mass. Fully 40,000 people were on the park at the time of starting the races, and the entire affair was a grand success.

Clearly the size of the crowd and the number of participants from all parts of the country stamped this event and others like it as attractions of national interest. But the spirit of the day, as the *Globe* attested, was in going to the track.

The scenes on the way to the track were worthy of the artist's sketch-book, for never has Puritanical New England been so fully represented on the road to the races. Extra trains were run by the Lowell road, which lands passengers at about one-eighth of a mile from the track, at "Brick Yard Crossing," and besides these, trains were run by the Main road on its Medford branch track, landing passengers about a third of a mile from the park gates. . . . Every style of wagon, carriage, chaise, buggy, stage-coach, omnibus, gig, sulky, or other vehicular conveyance could be seen in the queer procession that drew up before the ticket-takers at the gate. . . .

The press was well represented, the reporters of the city papers being largely outnumbered by the correspondents of the New York City press, the attachés of the sporting papers of the country, and "special commissioners" from nearly every prominent paper in the Union. The Franklin Telegraph wires were connected with the stand, and a special operator flashed the records of the contest to every city, from East to West and North to South.[8]

The image of this institution—America's first mass-supported and mass-endorsed spectator sport—appeared not only in paintings and lithographs but also in the form of weather vanes that adorned barns and homes. These marvelous devices, both commercially made and folk carved, are a decorative, material link between the rural America that begot the champions of the turf and the fast-rising urban society that exploited them.

The full flower of the Grand Circuit in the eighties and nineties caused the popularity of harness racing to burgeon. Gone were the days of jockey-club matches for gentlemanly wagers, the head-to-head encounters on Race Street in Philadelphia or along New York's Harlem Lane. The excitement of the midcentury agricultural-society fair was dwarfed by the commercial emphasis of the Grand Circuit. Broadsides that drummed coming events

8. *The Boston Daily Globe*, September 16, 1874.

on the Circuit—like the one included in this collection—were lithographed. The lithographer as the popular recorder and interpreter of a singularly American pastime was, despite ever greater takes at the turnstiles in every driving park, losing ground to the more immediate, novel, realistic, and accurate image captured by the cameraman and his lens. The folio portraits of horses and track scenes suffered increasingly from the impact of photography. The lithographic artist found the romance of the trotting turf stripped away by the harshness and accuracy of the still picture. This is reflected in such prints as Jay Eye See, a photo-oliograph horse portrait by Clay & Richmond, in E. Bosqui & Company's portrait of St. Julien, and in the Frontier Lithograph Co.'s rendition of Cresceus.

The aura of the trotting park is best suggested in the description of a four-day meet held at Hartford's Charter Oak Park between August 27 and 31 in 1889. *The Hartford Courant* gave the meet full coverage, and at the park itself "the accommodations for the public and the press were admirable. In the press stand an awning and a telephone communicating with the judges' stand was thoroughly appreciated." Unlike the early days, on the way out to the Long Island tracks or to Point Breeze Park "trains on both the New England and Consolidated roads brought crowds to Hartford." Nevertheless, some things fortunately remained unchanged despite technical advance. "Upon the grand stand were many ladies, and their handsome costumes made a very pretty picture." It was not the artist's sketchbook, however, that recorded the panorama of the park on this splendid day, but rather an array of "sundry photographers." The second day of the meet found the reporter still impressed by the lens and by "a photographer [who] placed his camera in the middle of the enclosure of the track." With the stands overflowing and "not a vacant seat to be seen," the picture being taken seemed likely to produce "a very inspiring scene." During the third day of the Grand Circuit race at Hartford, patronage continued high, and again "the grand stand was brilliant with the costumes of a great many ladies." And, as might be expected at Hartford, "Colt's band kept up to its usual high standard." The *Courant* on closing day could proudly boast that the past week had been one of the most successful in the history of Charter Oak Park.[9]

Thus briefly outlined from 1820 forward is the journey of the lithograph and the newspaper as they followed "the trotting turf" throughout the nineteenth century. It is a lively and spirited road and one which contrasts widely at times with the pessimistic and dull-brown view of American life in the Victorian Age. This is not to say that the reality of the day was the vivid hue of the printmaker. It is rather to suggest that in the trotting horse and track and the brief respite of leisure and enjoyment they provided, Americans found an escape. In part the motivation was pragmatic in that it was a manifestation of a much larger quest for speed, and in part it was idealistic in that it sought perfection in an animal that most persons thought uniquely American—the standardbred trotting horse.

It remained for a poet, Oliver Wendell Holmes, in an overview to place in perspective the graphic, literary, material, social, and psychological elements that combined to make up the history of harness racing between 1820 and 1900. On May 11, 1876, Holmes had attended the annual dinner of the editors of the *Harvard Advocate* which was that evening celebrating its tenth anniversary. Responding to a toast in place of the president of the university who was absent, Holmes spoke briefly about the literary achievements of the college during his undergraduate years, and "then, to the surprise and gratification of all" he produced a poem "prepared for the occasion." It was a sequel to the "Wonderful One-Hoss Shay," and its subject was the trotting horse. The title of the poem was "How the Old Horse Won the Bet," and of it the poet later wrote in 1891 that "unquestionably there is something a little like extravagance" in it, that he felt would indeed tax "the credulity of experienced horsemen." Still, in the history of horse racing, and particularly that of the trotting course, there had been "a good many surprises." It was to "those who have fol-

9. *The Hartford Courant*, August 28–August 31, 1889.

lowed the history of the American trotting horse" that the author turned for license, asking that they remember Dutchman, Old Blue, and the more recent marvels of speed and endurance like Maud S and her time of 2:08¾ set in 1885—this some nine years after the first appearance of Holmes' poem in the *Atlantic* (July 1876). Praising the admirable, self-perpetuating qualities of the trotting horse as opposed to the terminal, mechanistic perfection of the shay was seemingly the poet's purpose, and "if there are any anachronisms or other inaccuracies in this story" he asked that the event and not the details be remembered by his readers.

The trotting-horse prints, despite a basic sameness, when viewed individually engender some feeling either of action, competition, pride, nostalgia, or of status and quality. The same qualities are found in the literature of the period. All the excitement of the track on "a big day" is still viable in "How The Old Horse Won The Bet."[10] Both poet and print-maker responded to a common stimulus. The horse and race were the thing, and details from track to track and meet to meet often merged into the kind of standard view briskly set down by Holmes.

> 'T was on the famous trotting-ground,
> The betting men were gathered round
> From far and near; the "cracks" were there
> Whose deeds the sporting prints declare. . . .

Precisely as in the static and highly romanticized prints, anticipation mounts as Holmes recalls the splendid drivers and trainers of the period, past and present—Hiram Woodruff, Dan Pfeiffer [Pfifer], and Budd Doble—and offspring of the foundation of the American

---

10. See *The Harvard Advocate*, vol. 21 (May 26, 1876), p. 88, and Oliver Wendell Holmes, *The One Hoss Shay with its Companion Poems, How the Old Horse Won the Bet* . . . (Boston, 1892), pp. 5–6. Old Dutchman was one of the earliest trotting favorites, and Old Blue a particular Boston favorite of the early nineteenth century.

standardbred horse—Imported Messenger and Justin Morgan—assembled by literary license for the day's big event in the guise of Lady Suffolk, Dexter, and Goldsmith Maid.

The poet's romantic view of the track was almost nostalgic and was held nearly unanimously by painter, printmaker, and man of letters alike. It was a beautiful composite that the camera and more objective reporting would soon end:

> *Blue are the skies of opening day;*
> *The bordering turf is green with May;*
> *The sunshine's golden gleam is thrown*
> *On sorrell, chestnut, bay, and roan. . . .*

The gathering crowd at any track was also a standard array that differed little, whether in Boston, Philadelphia, New York, or at the myriad lesser tracks, rural or urban, throughout the middle decades of the century. In both poem and print the gradations of social status within these crowds is readily apparent from the style of equipage that conveyed them to the trotting grounds.

> *Wagons and gigs are ranged about,*
> *And fashion flaunts her gay turn-out;*
> *Here stands—each youthful Jehu's dream—*
> *The jointed tandem, ticklish team!*
> *And there in ampler breadth expand*
> *The splendors of the four-in-hand. . . .*

And, indeed, what the prints so often declare the poet confirms: the trotting turf was not exclusively for masculine enjoyment alone. Men and women from all walks of life came to the track. And many—just like their wagons or carriages—were decked in the height of fashion.

> *On faultless ties and glossy tiles*
> *The lovely bonnets beam their smiles;*
> *(The style's the man, so books avow;*

The style's the woman, anyhow);
From flounces frothed with creamy lace
Peeps out the pug-dog's smutty face,
Or spaniel rolls his liquid eye,
Or stares the wiry pet of Skye—
O woman, in your hours of ease
So shy with us, so free with these!

The pathos, tension, and climax of every match or meeting held since the sport had arisen in the 1820s was treated collectively in prints and by Holmes as well. Always there were the favorites, the tried and tested. Always the unproved was in the field, and always, too, the sentimental favorite, often tired but still full of heart. The poet, and occasionally the printmaker, championed the underdog. Holmes pitted the parson's nag against the best: Old Hiram's gray (Lady Suffolk), Pfeiffer's [Pfifer's] sorrel (Dexter), and Budd Doble's bay (Goldsmith Maid). The race itself, like those frequently pictured in the prints of the day or described in the press, was quite a match. The best that the American trotting turf had produced was "going under saddle" in the early style against the parson's bag of bones:

So worn, so lean in every limb,
It can't be they are saddling him!

The sentiment for the underdog builds as the old horse is saddled and mounted.

And so, his rider on his back,
They lead him, limping, to the track....

The crowd is scornful, some amused, some unbelieving; and, from the competition going to the start,

One pitying look old Hiram cast;
"Go it, ye cripple, while ye can!"

Smuggler. Haskell & Allen, Boston, 1874.

CHAS. S. HUMPHREYS, PINXT.   ENTERED ACCORDING TO ACT OF CONGRESS IN THE YEAR 1869 BY ALDEN GOLDSMITH IN THE CLERK'S OFFICE OF THE DISTRICT COURT OF THE U.S. FOR THE SOUTHERN DIST. OF NEW YORK.   PRINTED IN COLORS BY MAYER & MERKEL 184 FULTON ST. N.Y.

VOLUNTEER

SIRED BY RYSDYK'S HAMBLETONIAN, DAM BY YOUNG PATRIOT &c. &c.

PROPERTY OF ALDEN GOLDSMITH, BLOOMING GROVE, ORANGE CO. N.Y.

RYSDYK'S HAMBLETONIAN

HARTFORD RACES
CHARTER OAK PARK

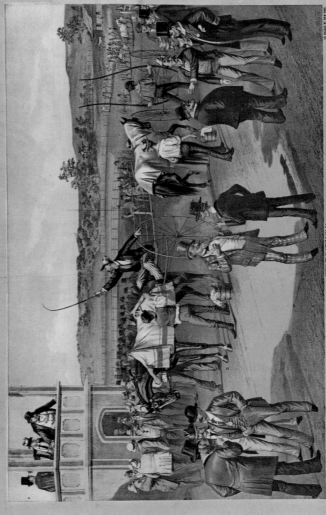

A GOOD RACE, WELL WON.

AUGUST 27, 28, 29, 30, 1889.

PREMIUMS $36,000.00

INCLUDING THE

$10,000.00 STAKE

FOR THE

WINNERS OF THE GRAND CIRCUS.

T. O. KING, Secretary.

CURRIER & IVES' ILLUSTRATED RACE POSTERS. 115 NASSAU STREET, NEW YORK.

> *Cried out unsentimental Dan;*
> *"A Fast-Day dinner for the crows!"*
> *Budd Doble's scoffing shout arose.*

But, as the old nag draws near the starting line, he remembers his past and his inheritance, the substance of which all trotters are made. This same substance the imagination of the artist and the printmaker always seems to portray. And suddenly:

> *"Go!"—Through his ear the summons stung*
> *As if a battle-trump had rung;*
> *The slumbering instincts long unstirred*
> *Start at the old familiar word. . . .*

The field is past the quarter pole. The crowd no longer laughs. And now, from Holmes' lines, is seen the classic view of the trotting horse delineated so often by the printmakers. With the field going at a full trot, the faster the old horse moved, the

> *Tighter his frightened jockey clung*
> *As in a mighty stride he swung,*
> *The gravel flying in his track,*
> *His neck stretched out, his ears laid back,*
> *His tail extended all the while*
> *Behind him like a rat-tail file!*

The pace increases. The young rider on the old nag is almost unseated. The best horses in the field now start to move—

> *And off they spring, and round they go,*
> *The fast ones doing "all they know!"*

But not for long, for the old warrior is setting too hot a pace. All the effort usually conserved for three heats is going into one. And what of the competition at such a clip?

They're tailing off! they're losing ground!
Budd Doble's nag begins to fail!
Dan Pfeiffer's sorrel whisks his tail!
And see! in spite of whip and shout,
Old Hiram's mare is giving out!

The impossible has happened: something no one could explain, a climax no one had anticipated. Again the verse recalls the lithographic view so familiar to the nineteenth-century sporting world:

Now for the finish! at the turn,
The old horse—all the rest astern—
Comes swinging in, with easy trot;
By Jove! he's distanced all the lot!

How could such an upset be explained? Had old Dutchman been reincarnated? Or, as Old Hiram suggested, was this unaccounted-for performance really the Devil's work? It was neither, confides the poet. Because, as any good trotting buff should know, this victory by the underdog was little more than Hiram Woodruff's firmest adage come to pass. What Woodruff, who had had no peer in trotting circles, so long propounded, Oliver Wendell Holmes revered. Simply then, remembering the long-lived performers who had dominated the sport within his memory span, the poet concluded that the

Moral for which this tale is told;
A horse can trot, for all he's old.[11]

The horses discussed and pictured in the chapters that follow preserve this very quality. They are never too old, for they perpetuate the excitement, the pride, and the relaxation that many Americans found at the track, on the road, and in that product of a splendid tribe, the American trotting horse.

11. Oliver Wendell Holmes, *The Poetical Works of Oliver Wendell Holmes* (Boston, 1880), pp. 309–311.

By 1868, when Hiram Woodruff wrote his memoir, the wagon and the sulky had replaced the jockey in saddle as the true test of speed and stamina for the trotting horse. At this late date the trotter was seldom ridden except at walking exercises or on his way to the black-smith shop. But this had not always been the case. Trotting horses at first raced under saddle in the same manner as thoroughbred runners. One of the earliest trotting prints in the Peters Collection is a lithograph by George Endicott, of New York, published about 1830, showing Columbus and Sally Miller competing in an under-saddle match. According to Hiram Woodruff there was an advantage to this mode of racing, for "when a horse is clever under the saddle, it is a better and faster way of going than in harness."[1] Woodruff thought that, when properly trained, very few horses ever trotted as fast in harness as with a jockey in the saddle. Woodruff wished for a return to the good old days of racing trotters under saddle, and he longed for the jock dressed in silks. The riders of trotters—as in the Endicott print—were always dressed as jockeys, and great expense was incurred in provid-ing them with rich velvets and silks of bright hue. The nostalgic Woodruff recalled the exploits of Columbus and his chief competitors thundering along "at the flying trot," un-doubtedly in much the same manner as shown in the lithograph.

The print of the dock-tailed Columbus preserves a portrait of the first horse to have trotted three miles in less than eight minutes, a feat he performed in 1833 and for which he was widely acclaimed.[2] Columbus was a bright bay gelding (though the Endicott print shows him as a black horse) some sixteen hands high, whose pedigree was unclear. Peter Whelan, his rider in the print, was one of the best known of the earlier trotting-horse jockeys. His prowess in handling trotters under saddle became legend as the century pro-gressed and this phase of horsemanship declined. Sally Miller's distinction was that she had trotted the fastest saddle time on record in 1832. Foaled in the 1820s, she was of sound

1. Hiram Woodruff, *The Trotting Horse of America* (New York, 1868), p. 275.   2. Ibid., p. 132.

TROTTERS UNDER SADDLE

COLUMBUS

AND
SALLA MILLER.
COLUMBUS, WINNER OF TWENTY-TWO MATCHES AND PURSES.

No. 1. Centreville, May 9th, 1830. Purse $300; 5 mile heats, under saddle, distanced Spot. Time 8m. 27½s. 2. Hunting Park, May 30th, 1830. Purse $200; 5 mile heats, under saddle, beat Ephraim Smooth, Top Gallant and Lady Jackson. Time 8m. 19s. 8m. 27s. 3. Centreville, May 6th, 1831. Purse $500; 3 mile heats, under saddle, beat Cato, Tyro and Sweetbriar. Time 5m. 3½s. 8m. 16s. 8m. 15s. 4. Centreville, October 8th, 1832. Purse $200; 3 mile heats, under saddle, distanced Betsy Baker, Jerry and Crazy Jane. Time 7s. 5. Hunting Park, October 18th, 1832. Purse $200; 2 mile heats, under saddle, beat "SALLY MILLER" and Comet. Time 5m. 22s. 5m. 21s. 6. Harlem, June 13th, 1833. Purse $200; heats thrice round, beat Collector and distanced Charley. Time 7m. 34s. 2. Course 109 yards, short of a mile. 7. Centreville, September 25th, 1833. Purse $300; 3 mile heats, under saddle, distanced Screw-driver and Collector. Time 8m. 14s. 8. Centreville, December 2d, 1833. Match, stakes $300, heats best 3 in 5, under saddle, beat Comet in 3 heats. Time —. —. 9. Hunting P. January 1st, 1834. Match, stakes $500, mile heats under saddle, beat Charlotte Temple in 2 heats. Time —. —. 10. Centreville, May 2d, 1834. Purse $300; 3 mile heats, under saddle, beat Charlotte Temple. Time 8m. 2s. 8m. 5s. 11. Hunting Park, May, 1834. Purse $300; 3 mile heats, under saddle, beat Lady Jackson and Screw-driver. Time 8m. 7s. 8m. 11s. 12. Harlem, June 25th, 1834. Purse $200; heats thrice round the Course, under saddle, beat Confidence and Charlotte Temple. Time 7m. 45s. 7m. 42s. 7m. 49s. 13. Centreville, October 3d, 1834. Purse $300; 3 mile heats, under saddle, beat Rolla. Time 8m. 5s. 8m. 6s. 14. Hunting Park, October, 1834. Purse $300; 3 mile heats, under saddle, beat Lady Jackson and Screw-driver in 2 heats. Time 7m. 57s. 8m. 3s. 15. Baltimore, ——, 1834. Purse $——; 5 mile heats, under saddle, beat Dread, Jackson and Spot. Time —. —. 16. Hunting Park, November 22d, 1834. Purse $200; 2 mile Centreville, October 1st, 1835. Purse $300; 3 mile heats, in harness, beat Rolla and Calvin Edson. Time 8m. 24½s. 8m. 20½s. 19. Trenton, April, 1835. P. ness, beat Rolla and Fanny Pullen. Time 8m. 15s. 8m. 24s. 21. Beacon Course, May 10th, 1838. Purse $200; 2 mile heats, under saddle, beat Daniel Webster under saddle, beat Dread. Time 5m. 23s. 5m. 47s. 17. Centreville, May 5th, 1835. Purse $300; 3 mile heats, under saddle, beat Rolla. Time 8m. 24s. 18. $200; 3 mile heats, under saddle, beat Top Gallant, Comet and Lady Jackson, in 2 heats. Time —. —. 20. Centreville, May 17th, 1836. Purse $300; 3 mile heats, in harness, beat 5m. 41s. 5m. 52. 22. Beacon Course, May 11th, 1838. Purse $200; mile heats best 3 in 5, under saddle, beat "Rattler." Time 2m. 47s. 2m. 46s. 2m. 47s. 2m. 46s.

RODE BY PETER WHELAN.

Painted by R.S. Hillman.

Childs & Inman Lith.

COLUMBUS.

trotting stock. Her sire was Mambrino, who looked directly to Imported Messenger as his sire and who himself was a progenitor of many fine trotters.

Richard Hillman documented in oil a trotting meet at Philadelphia's Hunting Park in 1831. It is the earliest known painting of a trotting match in the United States. The artist captured what by modern standards seems nearly a rural scene. It is one rich in fall colors, brightened by jockey silks and the appealing artistic grouping of the bays and whites. The Hillman painting serves as a prototype. Almost without exception, early lithographers who rendered prints of trotters under saddle repeated the gait, the jockey's seat, and the track surroundings in the manner portrayed by Hillman. Sometime between 1831 and 1833 Childs & Inman rendered their portrait of Columbus after a painting by Hillman, a sign, house, and decorative painter from Springfield, Illinois, who had also painted a portrait of Lady Suffolk. Trotting contests under saddle were often noted in the national press, and in October of 1832 the *National Gazette,* in Philadelphia, reported a trotting match at Hunting Park Course with Columbus, Sally Miller, and Comet contending for the purse. Columbus won both two-mile heats with a best time of 5:21. The event described in the *Gazette* may well have prompted the publication of the Childs & Inman lithograph.[3]

Lady Suffolk appears next in the chronological progression of under-saddle trotting prints in the Peters Collection. Harry T. Peters called this print, published by Lewis & Brown in 1844, "the best under saddle trotting lithograph of them all."[4] A viewer with very little imagination can conjure from it the exploits of this amazing horse on the trotting courses at Centreville, Beacon, Hunting Park, Union, and Cambridge. Frank Forester in his treatise on the American horse first published in 1857 used the lithograph as a faithful illustration of this splendid animal, whom he described as "about fifteen hands and a half

3. For Childs & Inman and Endicott, see Harry T. Peters, *America on Stone* (Garden City, N. Y., 1931), pp. 136–140, 171–180. For Hillman, see George C. Groce and David H. Wallace, *The New-York Historical Society's Dictionary of Artists in America 1564–1860* (New Haven, 1957), p. 317.   4. Peters, *America on Stone,* p. 265.

PAINTED BY ROBT A. CLARKE

Entered according to Act of Congress, in year 1844, n Robt A. Clarke, in the Clerks office of the District Court of the South dis't of New York

LITH OF LEWIS & BROWN, ST JOHN ST N.Y.

LADY SUFFOLK

THE CELEBRATED TROTTING MARE.

and her rider, Albert Concklin as they appeared on the BEACON COURSE, HOBOKEN, N.J. *on the 12th July, 1843.*

From an Original Painting by Robert A. Clarke, by whom this portrait is most respectfully dedicated to

Wm T Porter Esqr of N. York

[66]

Painted by Robt. A. Clarke   Entered according to act of congress in the year 1843, by G. W. Lewis, in the clerks office of the southern district of New York.   Lith of G. W. Lewis, 122 Fulton Street N.Y.

LADY SUFFOLK

THE CELEBRATED TROTTING MARE.

Foaled in 1833. Died 7 March, 1855.

and her rider, ALBERT CONCKLIN, as they appeared on the BEACON COURSE, HOBOKEN, N.J. on the 12 July 1843;

from an original painting by ROBᵗ A. CLARKE, by whom this portrait is most respectfully dedicated to

Wm T. Porter Esq. of N. York

60.355

high; of a beautiful gray, with a large sweeping tail; small head, well set on to a fine arched neck, with a good deal of the Arab about it; large shoulders and quarters, not too heavy, but showing immense strength and power of endurance; long in the body, legs fine and wonderfully good."[5]

The Lewis & Brown portrait of Lady Suffolk was dedicated to publisher William T. Porter, Esq. It shows the talented jockey, Albert Conklin, and Lady Suffolk presumably as they appeared at Beacon Course at Hoboken, New Jersey, on July 12, 1843. The *New York Daily Tribune* of July 13 reported that the day before had seen the Course at Hoboken "thronged with the gentry of the turf." The crowd on this day witnessed the fastest time thus far recorded in a trotting match. In the very first heat the gray mare from Long Island reduced by five seconds the old mark made by Edwin Forest in 1834. She crossed the line in 2:26½ flat, finishing ahead of Beppo and a pacer named Oneida Chief (ridden in this race by none other than Hiram Woodruff). Lady Suffolk had become trotting's first 2:30 or better miler, and in so doing she became "mistress of the trotting turf." Bred in Suffolk County, Long Island, and foaled in 1833, Lady Suffolk entered her first trotting race at Babylon, New York, in 1838, ridden by Hiram Woodruff. Between 1838 and 1854 she trotted in 161 races, winning 88, losing 73, and accumulating over $35,000 in prize money. Lady Suffolk was not simply a local favorite, and during her racing career she appeared in most major cities from Boston to New Orleans. When she died in 1855 William Porter, to whom the Lewis & Brown print was dedicated, published in his *The Spirit of the Times*—the most widely read sporting journal of the day—a touching obituary which ended simply: "We shall see the gray mare no more." The finality of Lady Suffolk's obituary was mitigated to a degree at least by Lewis & Brown's lithograph.[6]

---

5. Henry William Herbert [Frank Forester], *Frank Forester's Horse and Horsemanship of the United States and the British Provinces of North America* (New York, 1871), vol. 2, p. 208. Hereafter cited *Frank Forester*. 6. *The Spirit of the Times*, June 2, 1855.

Trotters under Saddle   Lady Suffolk's popularity can be judged by the number of prints that depicted her. In addition to the one just discussed, four others are preserved in the Peters Collection. One is similar in every detail to the Lewis and Brown version of the Robert Clarke painting, but it is without letters and differs in color. In 1857 George W. Lewis, of New York, published a colored lithograph, again after the portrait by Robert A. Clarke. By vignetting the older version of this print in the manner of a commemorative with birth and death dates added, Lewis continued to trade on the popularity of Lady Suffolk. This, despite the fact that her record had been reduced a full second by Tacony in 1853 and yet another second by Flora Temple in 1856! As in the earlier Lewis print, Conklin is shown aboard Lady Suffolk winning at Beacon Course. Another print without caption appears to be certainly a portrait of the Old Gray Mare. The flowing tail and the long muscular body are unquestionably that of Lady Suffolk. In this print the rider in profile seems to be an in-saddle portrait of Hiram Woodruff. Despite the inference of the successive prints commemorating her exploits, it was a fact that in her last six years on the track (1847–1853) the Old Gray Mare was infrequently raced under saddle. The sulky and the wagon had become more popular tests of speed and endurance. In the 161 recorded races of her career Lady Suffolk trotted under saddle 44 times, but only seven of these occasions occurred after 1847.[7]

The last of the Lady Suffolk prints is a late form of the lithograph, a trade card copyrighted in 1889 by Kinney Bros., makers of "High-Class Cigarettes." The advertisement is an indication of the lasting fame of the Old Gray Mare from Long Island. David Bryant is the jockey pictured in the saddle. Bryant had purchased Lady Suffolk as a two-year-old in 1835, and the two were together until 1851 when Bryant died. Frank Forester, romantic, sentimental, and a true lover of horses, saw Lady Suffolk's loss of Bryant as the loss of "an intimate friend." The old horse, according to Forester, was never quite the same again. It

7. *Frank Forester*, vol. 2, pp. 208–212.

Untitled [Lady Suffolk].

LADY SUFFOLK,

The Renowned Gray Mare, Record 2:26 Ridden by David Bryant.

COPYRIGHTED 1889. —— *Kinney Bros* —— HIGH CLASS CIGARETTES.

by R.A. Clarke.   Entered according to act of Congress in the year 1856 by E.K.Conklin in the Clerks Office of the District Court of the Eastern District of Pennsylvania.   Lith by W.H.Rease 97 Chestnut St. Phila.

Lady Suffolk.   Zachary Taylor.   Tacony.   Mac.   Jack Rossiter.   Lady Moscow.   Flora Temple.   Highland Maid.

CELEBRATED AMERICAN TROTTING HORSES.

Printed by Wagner & M. Guigan.

should be remembered that Lady Suffolk's best time for the mile was 2:26½, and that, despite the impression given by the advertisement, she had on this occasion been ridden, not by Bryant, but rather by Albert Conklin.

Included in the Peters Collection of trotting horses under saddle is a black-and-white lithograph, "Celebrated American Trotting Horses," by W. H. Rease, of Philadelphia, again after a painting by Robert Clarke. An Irish immigrant and a painter of animals, Clarke came to America about 1834. He settled first in New York and later, in about 1850, moved to Philadelphia. His work was exhibited by the American Art Union and at the Pennsylvania Academy. His prize rendering of a trotter had been, as we have seen, a portrait of Lady Suffolk, whom he now grouped with a new generation of trotting celebrities in this composite print. Frank Forester admired the spirited work of Clarke. According to Forester, Clarke had a talent of catching and putting on paper the action and style of movement and the salient characteristics of any horse in motion—this particularly of horses at the trot. Historically, the Rease print suggests that for turfmen of the 1850s the saddle still lingered as a popular mode of racing trotters. The print is also a reminder of the great popularity and appeal of the American trotting horse.[8] No description in the caption of this print was needed; the buyer knew at first glance Lady Suffolk's identity. Zachary Taylor, Tacony, Mac, Jack Rossiter, Flora Temple, and Highland Maid, all of whom are shown in this print, were equally familiar to the sporting public. By this date most of these horses had gained distinction by regularly beating the tired and worn Lady Suffolk. The print represented what Frank Forester called the new era of the American trotting turf. The great competitors of the thirties and forties, symbolized by the Old Gray Mare, were gone, and many, like Columbus and Sally Miller, were forgotten. Of the new celebrities in 1854, Flora Temple's fame would be the most lasting. Her matches—with Hiram Woodruff most

8. For Rease, see Peters, *America on Stone*, pp. 331–332; for Clarke, see Groce and Wallace, *New-York Historical Society's Dictionary of Artists*, pp. 129–130.

often her driver—against Highland Maid, Mac, and Tacony were newsworthy sporting events of the 1850s.

The last in-saddle trotter portrait in the Peters Collection is of Dexter, here ridden by Budd Doble. Dexter's markings were distinctive. He was a very rich-brown gelding with a blaze on his face and four white legs, qualities well shown in the print. The print itself is interesting, for it is a colored combination lithograph and photograph. Dexter followed Flora Temple as the country's outstanding trotter. As Flora had dominated the 1850s and early 1860s, so Dexter met and overcame most challengers between 1864 and 1867. Writing in 1868 from firsthand knowledge and experience, Woodruff could scarcely conceive that there had ever been a better trotting horse than Dexter. He had all the qualities and traits that a good trotter requires. He was amazingly fast and strong as well. He could go the course under saddle, he could go it in harness, or, if need be, he could go it hitched to a wagon. According to Woodruff, Dexter was equally good on a hard track and in the mud, and, finally and most important, he was "a grand campaigner." To Woodruff he appeared always "very resolute and workmanlike." Dexter was foaled in Orange County, New York, having been sired by Rysdyk's Hambletonian, the greatest progenitor of trotting flesh ever put to stud. On August 14, 1867, at Buffalo in a harness trot against time, Dexter negotiated the mile in the record time of $2:17\frac{1}{4}$. After this feat he was purchased by Robert Bonner. The sporting public regretted the retirement of this splendid champion, and the *American Agriculturist*, which at an earlier date had bitterly fought the encroachment of the trotting track at agricultural fairs, now wrote with despair of the retirement by Bonner of a horse of such unprecedented power, speed, and with such immense promise of a brilliant career.[9]

Dexter's marvelous speed was, of course, his claim to fame; in addition, however, he ended the mid-nineteenth-century prejudice that prevailed against white-legged horses:

9. Woodruff, *Trotting Horse*, pp. 347–348; *American Agriculturist*, vol. 27 (October 1868: new series), p. 368.

"DEXTER."

Ridden by Mr. BUDD DOBLE.

FOALED APRIL, 1858.   RECORD 2:17¼.   DIED APRIL, 1888.

One white leg, inspect him;
Two white legs, reject him;
Three white legs, sell him to your foes;
Four white legs, feed him to the crows!

In Dexter's day trotters in harness—either to sulky or wagon—were the standard fare on the racing circuit. The saddle riding of trotters had for many years been neglected, but for a brief time the style was revived, and Budd Doble was among the most adept riders. Woodruff thought Doble a superb horseman, and he wrote in his memoir that Doble had given the turf followers "specimens of saddle-horsemanship" reminiscent of the days when the sport was in its infancy. The scene depicted in this print appears to be Dexter and Doble finishing in front of the clubhouse at Point Breeze Park in Philadelphia.[10]

Good roads and improved wagons caused the general decline of the saddle horse as a practical means of conveyance. By midcentury few travelers in the northeastern and middle states faced the rigors of the saddle. The track reflects the shift of emphasis seen in routine travel from horseback to wagon or sulky. Indeed, there is a direct correlation between the improved modes of transportation and their popular manifestation seen on trotting tracks. To a nostalgic horseman and trainer, however, such relationships were unimportant. For Hiram Woodruff in his declining years it was important only that the current crop of trotting stalwarts would surely have been much faster "if they had been accustomed to trot under the saddle." The in-saddle prints of trotters on the track preserved in the Peters Collection do little to prove Woodruff right or wrong; they do, however, document a racing style now nearly forgotten.

10. Woodruff, *Trotting Horse*, pp. 276, 348; for Point Breeze Park, see Nicholas B. Wainwright, *Philadelphia in the Romantic Age of Lithography* (Philadelphia, 1958), pp. 187–188.

Whalebone

A Noted Horse for Speed & Bottom. Bright bay, 15 hands 3½ inches high, has strong points & shews great blood, was sired by Hamiltonian & Hamiltonian by old Messenger. He was bred by General Coles of Long Island. Amongst his numerous performances are the following, 1827 —
He was matched on the New York trotting Course against time 15 miles within the hour in harness which he accomplished in 54 minutes & 6 seconds with great ease performing his last mile in 3 minutes & 2 seconds his then owner M.ᶜ Elliott after the match offered to trot him 17 miles
within the hour but was not taken up.   May 15, 1828, won the Hunting park Association purse of $200, & a silver Cup value $50. beating in two heats, Cropper, Lady Kate, Grey Squirrel & Moonshine.   October 15, 1829. on the Hunting park Association Course he trotted under the Saddle
rode by M.ᶜ Spicer 16 miles in 4 mile heats in the unprecedented time of 44 minutes & 7seconds, performing the third heat in 11 minutes & 19seconds, the day previous he trotted 8 miles in harness against Sir Peter)   October 23, 1830, won the Hunting Park Association Purse of $300.
3 mile heats winning the 3.ᵈ & 4.ᵗʰ heats, beating Sir Peter, Jerry, Comet, & Top Gallant, and distancing all on the 4.ᵗʰ heat.   October 28.ᵗʰ 1830, On the Union Course Long Island, he won the trotting Club purse of $200, beating the Colt, Camel, & Sir Andrew, winning the 2.ᵈ & 3.ᵈ heats the
Colt taking the first.   December 6, 1830, He beat Sweet Brier in Harness 7 miles round the Hunting Park Course, winning each mile except the 2.ᵈ & 5.ᵗʰ   On the New York trotting Course Dec.ʳ 1828, he performed a 2.ᵈ 3 mile heat in harness in 8 minutes 2 seconds
And on the Hunting Park Course October 14.ᵗʰ 1829, a second 1 mile heat in harness in 4 minutes 1 seconds, and is fully considered the best bottomed horse in the Country.

The *American Agriculturist* in 1883 pointed out to its readers that "the light trotting sulky made of tough hickory and provided with light steel springs has been a leading cause of the present development of the trotter." Vehicles so constructed were of relatively recent vintage and had appeared first in eastern cities about 1845. In the minds of nineteenth-century writers, however, there was no doubt of causal relationships: "The perfecting of the vehicle and that of the horse have gone on together."[1] The Peters Collection preserves fourteen prints of trotters harnessed to sulkies. These date between 1830 and 1884, effectively spanning the great age of lithography and the first great age of enthusiasm for the trotting horse.

About 1830 Kennedy & Lucas of Philadelphia published a black-and-white lithograph drawn on stone by Richard Hillman that shows Whalebone, a great trotter, hitched to the earliest type of high, box-seated sulky. It was the sulky that brought a functional dimension to the racing of trotting horses. To speed and endurance first tested under saddle was added pulling power, a characteristic which had practical application to both rural and urban transportation. The harness prints trace chronologically the development of the sulky from a box hung on poles through the tough hickory-framed and steel-spring version, stopping just short of the bicycle-inspired, pneumatic-tired rig developed by the Tennessean Ed Geers in 1892. The rare view of Whalebone is the earliest of the harness portraits in the Peters Collection. It is unique among in-harness prints, for here is the first in a series of lively and spirited documents which attest the appearance, growing popularity, and near perfection of a singularly American sport. Whalebone, a fine-blooded bay gelding foaled in New York about 1821, was sired by Hambletonian by Imported Messenger. Hiram Woodruff recalled Whalebone as a "remarkably handsome horse," despite the fact that "he had but one eye." On a wet and muddy Long Island trotting course in

1. *American Agriculturist,* vol. 42 (August 1883), p. 355.

April 1827, Whalebone, in harness and against time, trotted 15 miles in 56 minutes. In 1831 he covered 32 miles in slightly over 1 hour and 58 minutes. This emphasis on stamina combined with speed marked Whalebone's career.[2]

After Whalebone, the harness portraits next document Sherman Black Hawk, who in October of 1856, competing against horses from all parts of the United States, took the first premium at the United States Agricultural Fair held at West Philadelphia. The event is commemorated in John Bufford's black-and-white lithograph after a painting by Charles S. Humphreys. In 1857 D. C. Linsley described Sherman Black Hawk as "jet black with [a] small star in his forehead." Linsley seldom found fault with the Morgan breed. He commended Sherman as a very spirited but tractable, compact, and well-made horse, and, like most Morgans, one that moved "in fine style."[3] At the Powelton Grounds in West Philadelphia in 1856, the site of the Fourth United States Agricultural Society Fair, Sherman Black Hawk showed his mettle. In Philadelphia *The Daily News* billed the race as "a trial of single horses, for speed." On the day of the race fifty thousand fairgoers were on the grounds, and the main attraction was "unquestionably the track." Large open stands (visible in the Bufford print) had been erected on the west side of the racecourse. Seating capacity was about eight thousand, and on this occasion the stands were thronged with expectant spectators. The infield also had filled rapidly, and at about three in the afternoon the entire scene was described as beautiful.[4]

2. Hiram Woodruff, *The Trotting Horse of America* (New York, 1868), pp. 129–130; Henry William Herbert [Frank Forester], *Frank Forester's Horse and Horsemanship of the United States and the British Provinces of North America* (New York, 1871), vol. 2, p. 139; hereafter cited *Frank Forester*. The catalog of W. A. Snow Iron Works of Chelsea, Mass. (ca. 1910), p. 85, illustrates a gilded-copper weather vane depicting Nancy Hanks hitched to a "pneumatic tire sulky," an interesting example of technical change manifesting itself rapidly in a purely decorative device. For Kennedy & Lucas, see Harry T. Peters, *America on Stone* (Garden City, N. Y., 1931), p. 249. 3. D. C. Linsley, *Morgan Horses* (New York, 1857), p. 311; for John H. Bufford, see Peters, *America on Stone*, pp. 118–127. 4. *The Daily News* (Philadelphia), October 9, 1856.

SHERMAN BLACK HAWK.

APPEARED, AT THE U.S. AGRICULTURAL FAIR, HELD AT WEST PHIL.ᵃ OCT.ᵗ 8.ᵗʰ 1856 AND TOOK THE FIRST PREMIUM, OF $200.ᵒᵒ COMPETING WITH HORSES FROM ALL PARTS OF THE UNITED STATES.

Sherman Black Hawk foaled May 30, 1843, the property of B.J. Myrick, Bridport Vt.

PEDIGREE. Sire. VERMONT BLACK HAWK, Dam. by YOUNG HAMILTONIAN, he by Dunham's HAMILTONIAN, by imported MESSINGER, Grand Dam. by imported MATCHUM. SHERMAN BLACKHAWK, is now owned by D. A. BENNETT, Bridport Vt., and DORA WARREN, Worcester Mass.

POINT BREEZE PARK,

Humphreys' portrait of Black Hawk, with Woodruff in the seat, suggests clearly that the trotting match was the high point of the agricultural fair, and this emphasis caused many agriculturists to grumble that the purpose of such fairs was distorted and usurped by a frantic devotion to "trials of speed," and this while the really important things were crowded into "some out-of-the-way corner, tent or building."[5] The purists had no sympathy with the racecourse in any shape or form. They felt, in brief, that an agricultural fair was not a time or place appropriate for such sport. Prints like Sherman Black Hawk are an index to the attitude which finally prevailed, and most visitors to the Powelton Grounds undoubtedly shared the view that "the trotting was very good."[6] Nicholas B. Wainwright, in his *Philadelphia in the Romantic Age of Lithography,* also records a colored print by P. S. Duvall & Company of the U. S. Agricultural Fair in 1856.[7]

Philadelphians first had witnessed pacing and trotting matches along Race Street, and the city's first formal trotting matches had been held on the Hunting Park Course as early as May of 1828. Thomas Sinclair in about 1855 published a colored lithograph after a drawing from nature by James Queen showing Point Breeze Park, which at the time was the newest of the Philadelphia trotting courses, having been completed in June of 1855. Point Breeze was on the Penrose Ferry Bridge Road, south of the city on the Schuylkill. The park proper was enclosed with a substantial fence which screened the clubhouse—a handsome brick building two stories high with a frontage of 125 feet. The building had a piazza which extended entirely around it and from which the entire track could be viewed by visitors.[8] Sinclair's lively print preserves the genteel aspects of trotting as a sport. It is

5. *American Agriculturist,* vol. 16 (November, 1857), p. 247. 6. *The Daily News* (Philadelphia), October 9, 1856. 7. Nicholas B. Wainwright, *Philadelphia in the Romantic Age of Lithography* (Philadelphia, 1958), p. 198. 8. See *Frank Forester,* vol. 2, pp. 140–142, for articles governing The Hunting Park Association in 1828; John H. Wallace, *The Horse of America* (New York, 1897), p. 179; and the *Public Ledger* (Philadelphia), June 21, 1855.

also an excellent example of the work of James Queen, whose brother owned the *Sporting Times*, the earliest of the sporting journals. Wainwright records this print as a sheet-music cover entitled "Point Breeze Park Shottisch."[9]

In 1865 Samuel Emerson, at the Riverside Riding Park in Brighton, together with Bufford & Sons, published a colored lithograph that showed the trotter Captain McGowan as he appeared in the twentieth mile of his greatest race. John Wallace, the foremost student of trotting-horse lineage in the nineteenth century, would not vouch for Captain McGowan's pedigree, and he records only that this roan gelding was bred in Kentucky and that he was "willful and bad tempered."[10] On the great occasion pictured in the lithograph Captain McGowan was driven by J. J. Bowen and had been trained for the event by J. E. Lawrence. Bowen's weight was 155 pounds, and the sulky pictured in the print weighed 70 pounds. Such a trial of speed and endurance had never before been attempted on a half-mile track, and press reports of the event were full of color, information, and excitement. Reporters all began their stories with the announcement of the record-breaking and unprecedented time that McGowan had turned in: twenty miles in 56 minutes and 25 seconds! McGowan's feat was witnessed by a crowd numbering between five and six thousand persons, among whom were horse lovers from New York and many other states. Betting was heavy, and in the stands many people stated loudly that no horse could accomplish the feat that McGowan had set for himself. Informed turfmen were certain that the gelding would break down before he had trotted fifteen miles. But his backers were confident, and in the fashion of the track they put up their money and took all bets that were offered.[11]

Moments before post time Captain McGowan appeared on the track harnessed to a very light gig with Bowen, who was reputed to be a careful driver, in the seat. The judges

9. See Peters, *America on Stone*, pp. 329, 367–369; Wainwright, *Philadelphia*, pp. 187–188.   10. Wallace, *Horse of America*, pp. 432–433.   11. *Boston Daily Advertiser*, November 1, 1865.

THE FAMOUS ROAN HORSE CAPT MC GOWAN AS HE APPEARED IN HIS 20TH MILE

IN HIS GREAT MATCH AGAINST TIME OF TROTTING IN HARNESS 20 MILES IN ONE HOUR WHICH HE ACCOMPLISHED IN 58 MINUTES AND 25 SECONDS

BEING THE FASTEST TIME ON RECORD OVER THE RIVER SIDE PARK, BRIGHTON, MASS. OCT. 31ST 1865

gave the word, and the horse started off at once. Bowen held him in for the first ten miles, at the end of which he appeared as fresh as when he began. No urging was needed to keep the horse to his task as he completed the first fifteen miles. During the seventeenth mile he broke for the first time, but his driver brought him back quickly. With the finish in sight people whispered that the sixth mile had been the Captain's best, trotted in a time of 2:43½ seconds. Near the end of the race the crowd, which had remained very quiet throughout the trot, cheered lustily as Captain McGowan came down the homestretch for the last time. When it was all over they flocked around the gelding and, in examining him, found no sign of injury. All afternoon it had been threatening rain, but despite the heavy clouds "it luckily did not fall until the trot was over." Trotting twenty miles in an hour on a half-mile course had never before been accomplished. Trustee and Lady Fulton, the only animals among a great number of American and European horses that had performed the feat on a mile track, had required more time to trot the distance than had Captain McGowan, and both had died soon after running this grueling distance. "Captain McGowan," crowed the press, "is not dead yet." Fifteen minutes after the race he was back on the track where he walked up and down and showed no ill effects; Captain McGowan had successfully demonstrated the desired qualities of endurance and speed. His owners, as a result, had collected a purse of $5500, and printmakers had gained subject matter for a portrait that was certain to achieve wide popular appeal.[12]

One of the most notable events of trotting-horse history occurred at the Fashion Course on Long Island, June 21, 1867. On that day Dexter trotted against Ethan Allen and his mate, a meeting documented well after the fact by Haskell & Allen of Boston in 1872. The day after Dexter met the pair *The New York Times* reported that "racing seems to be gradually becoming a sort of mania with a very considerable portion of our people."

12. Ibid.

The running horses that raced regularly at Jerome Park had not "excited anything like the enthusiasm which a genuine trot awakens on the Long Island Course." The *Times'* statement is not surprising, because the day before two of the century's greatest trotters had competed in one of their most memorable matches before a crowd of nearly fifteen thousand spectators.[13] Haskell & Allen's vivid version of this confrontation of trotting giants is even more lively and colorful when paired with descriptions by Charles Foster and John Wallace, both of whom saw the race. Charlotte F., Ethan Allen's usual running mate, was lame on this June day, and Ethan had been paired with a running horse, a Connecticut mare, in her place "to excite his ambition and induce him to do his best."[14] Despite this, however, the supposedly knowing bettors felt that the odds were two to one in favor of Dexter. Wallace récalled the vast crowd and the incalculable number of vehicles drawn up around the course. He remembered, too, the great applause when Dexter and Budd Doble came out and took their position at the pole.[15] Charles Foster, like Frank Forester, was a transplanted Englishman, having emigrated to the United States in 1847. He edited Hiram Woodruff's *Trotting Horse of America*, wrote for the *Spirit of the Times*, and was generally considered the best informed man in the country on the subject of racing. Wise in the ways of trotting turf, Foster knew Dexter was the underdog, and from this point of view he called the race and analyzed its result. The speed was amazing. At the quarter pole the double team was two lengths ahead. The fast pace was maintained as they went to the half-mile post with the pair now in front by three lengths. In the stretch the lead was widened to four, and at the finish line they had beaten Dexter by a full five lengths in the time of 2:15. It was a wonderful performance, but especially for Dexter, who had trotted singly and pulled his own vehicle and driver.

Betting at the beginning of the second heat was even, but well-informed observers

13. *The New York Times*, June 22, 1867.   14. *American Agriculturist*, vol. 27 (October 1868), p. 368.   15. Wallace, *Horse of America*, pp. 384–385.

DEXTER, ETHAN ALLEN AND MATE

AS THEY APPEARED AT FASHION COURSE L.I., JUNE 21ᵗʰ 1867 FOR A PURSE OF $ 2000.

TIME 2.15, 2.16, 2.19.

Publ. by Thomas Kelly 35 Bowery, N.Y.

PRINTED BY Wm. C. ROBERTSON 99 PEARL ST NY.

DEXTER, ETHAN ALLEN AND MATE

As they appeared at Morristown, N.J. July 4th 1867 for a Purse of $ 3,500.

TIME: 2.20½ 2.20½ 2.20.

thought the team might give out before the end of the third. The wise money was confident that Dexter would stay all the way. At the beginning of the second heat Ethan Allen broke. Dexter took the lead at the turn, trotting close to the outside. He had moved to the pole before he reached the quarter mark and still led at the end of the half mile, which he turned in 1:06. But by then Ethan Allen and his running mate had closed the gap, coming through the backstretch at full clip. The pace was so brisk that Ethan broke again on the turn, but the running mare caught him up quickly and he came back to the trot. Dexter was caught and beaten at the wire by three lengths in the good time of 2:16. Dexter's performance had been magnificent. It was probably a trotter's most notable example of "constancy and courage." In the third heat the team won again, this time in 2:19. Although defeated, Dexter's performance in this race settled three things. First, great as his powers were, they had simply been underrated. Second, no trotter on equal terms would have had a chance to beat him. And, third, a race between a trotter in single harness against another with a running mate was not a fair match. The result as analyzed was simple. Ethan Allen had not beaten Dexter—the running horse had done that.[16]

In this race were the two best trotters of the 1850s and 1860s. Dexter, foaled in 1858, had been sired by Rysdyk's Hambletonian. He was characterized by the blaze on his face and by his four white stockings. On the turf, however, it was not his conformation but his "arrow-like speed" that made him so well known. Ethan Allen, a stallion foaled in 1849, had an illustrious ancestry that included Black Hawk, Justin Morgan, and Imported Messenger. He was a bright bay with three white feet, a star on his forehead, and a flowing black tail. A sensation for eighteen trotting seasons, he was better perhaps longer than any other trotter. The usually objective John Wallace was moved to hyperbole by "his won-

16. Woodruff, *Trotting Horse*, pp. 407–408.

derful beauty and remarkable docility and kindness [and by] . . . the elegance and ease of his action." His trotting gait was recognized by all expert observers as probably the most perfect of any horse of his time. The printmakers made Ethan Allen and Dexter prime stars in the equine gallery, and so great was the pair's popularity that the match depicted in the lithograph by Haskell & Allen still stirred the turf enthusiast's blood as late as five years after the event in 1872.[17] Significantly, even well into the twentieth century weather-vane manufacturers made and advertised in their catalogs gilded-metal images of this indomitable pair of trotters and it is a safe assumption that a good many persons owned trotting-horse weather vanes and had them mounted above their stables or carriage houses. In 1875 J. W. Fiske of New York published a trade catalog that offered the public eight named weather vanes, trotters made of copper and gilded with gold leaf. Fiske billed himself as the oldest manufacturer of weather vanes in the United States. Prices for his copper trotters ranged from $75 for a 57-inch-long "Dexter" hitched to a sulky down to $15 for a free-standing unhitched "Ethan Allen Jr." that was 26 inches in length.

L. W. Cushing & Sons of Waltham, Massachusetts, in their catalog of 1883 offered fifteen general choices of trotter weather vanes. As in Fiske's catalog, each of Cushing's entries was named and illustrated and came in assorted sizes. The largest and most expensive was a 50-inch version of Ethan Allen hitched to a wagon. For this three-dimensional copper-and-gilt portrait Cushing asked $100. The weather vane, therefore, in addition to giving a clue to its owner's interests, was also an indication of status. For the less affluent— the person who wished for but could not afford even a $15 weather vane—there was the alternative of making one himself, thus producing in wood or sheet iron an object more truly folk in character than the factory-made versions offered by Fiske and Cushing.

Soon after their first encounter, Dexter met Ethan Allen and his mate again, this time on July 4, 1867, at Morristown, New Jersey, for a purse of $3500. Thomas Kelly, of New

17. *Frank Forester*, vol. 2, pp. 104–105, 253; Wallace, *Horse of America*, p. 381.

York, recorded this race in a colored lithograph published in 1868. Again Dexter and his driver, Budd Doble, tried valiantly to beat Ethan Allen and his driver, Dan Mace, this time with Ethan's regular mate, Charlotte F., running beside him. The purse, interestingly enough, was put up by the Morris County Agricultural Society. The occasion was what the urbane *New York Daily Tribune* called a "farmer's festival." The Morristown track was a half-mile oval with two straightaways of "forty rods each and two curves of the same length." It was not a favorable course for fast time; the curves were too sharp and "the straight going too short." The day was fine but hot, and the trot itself "as great a one as that at Fashion Course" held two weeks earlier.[18] The prospect of seeing Dexter in harness competing against Ethan Allen and Charlotte F. hitched to wagon had attracted "about 3000 persons," and on all sides the excitement was very great. The betting, although limited, was $100 to $50 on Ethan Allen and his mate. As at Fashion earlier, each heat was closely contested, with the difference of only a half second in the three heats! The aggregate time was 7 minutes and ¾ of a second. The team once again won in three straight heats: the first by a length, the second by three, and the third by a length, with times respectively, 2:20½, 2:20¼, and 2:20 flat. On a half-mile track these times were regarded as equal to, if not surpassing, the record set by the two horses on the Fashion Course.[19] By September 1867 Dexter had been purchased and retired by Robert Bonner. For the next twenty years he was a prize roadster in the Bonner stable. Ethan Allen lived until 1876, and as a sire he passed on the splendid Morgan characteristics which he had carried from the East to the plains of Kansas where he died.

Another Haskell & Allen print—this time of Smuggler—depicted "the long-heralded and famous contest which was to decide the title of the fastest trotting stallion in the United States."[20] The event took place at Boston's Mystic Park on September 15, 1874, and

18. *New York Daily Tribune*, July 6, 1867. For Thomas Kelly, see Peters, *America on Stone*, pp. 248–249.   19. *Daily State Gazette* (Trenton), July 6, 1867.   20. *Boston Daily Advertiser*, September 16, 1874.

it measured up to the expectations of the most exacting horsemen. Quick to seize an opportunity Haskell & Allen promptly issued this bright and spirited portrait of the winning animal and his driver, Charles Marvin. It was a banner day at Mystic Park. The track was in superb condition, and all the horses had been well trained and were in high spirits. The race had attracted what seemed the largest crowd thus far assembled on any trotting track, and prideful New England track goers felt certain that "the scene must have been something very like the Derby day." What the printmaker and the press proclaimed on this bright fall day in New England was the spectacle of a trotting match on the Grand Circuit in the heyday of the trotting turf. In the 1870s the quest for speed and new record times prevailed over the old horse-to-horse rivalries and competitions between owners. An urban East was enjoying urban leisure, and a Boston newspaper man captured the rush, crush, and expectancy of the day. "Teams," he wrote, "began to pour out from the city toward Medford as early as noon, and from that time until three o'clock a steady stream of conveyances of every description moved over the hill and along the dusty road—for it was dusty, although it had been watered—out to the track." In the city proper on the afternoon of the race there was scarely a hack left, nor a horse, nor a carriage of any kind for hire, "even a funeral would have had to be postponed." Twenty railroad cars on the Lowell line carried two thousand persons to the track, and some three thousand carriages on one road alone converged on Mystic Park. Once inside, "it was difficult to drive a horse without trampling someone under foot." The grandstand held about six thousand persons, and it was filled completely. Wherever a vacant spot occurred people filled it. Carriages lined the course all the way to the turn on each side of the track. The day was not merely for the gentry alone, however. A throng of humanity made up of "all sorts and all classes of people" had come to the race from all parts of the country and even from Canada. It was estimated that at least forty thousand trotting buffs saw Smuggler win the $10,000 purse.

After 1870 the scene at Mystic Park might well have been any of the stops on the Grand

Circuit—Cleveland's Driving Park; Hampdon Park at Springfield, Massachusetts; the Buffalo Driving Park; or the tracks at Poughkeepsie, Hartford, or Rochester. At one of these the track-goer might have seen Smuggler go against any of his principal rivals—Goldsmith Maid, Rarus, Mambrino Pilot, Great Eastern, or Judge Fullerton, to name but a few. Between 1870 and 1884 these animals and their assault on time records were publicized by the printmakers.[21]

Haskell & Allen kept their portrait of Smuggler current by adding to the print's original caption the times, places, and dates of his notable showings through the year 1876. Singular among these was a new mile mark for stallions set at Hartford on August 31, 1876. There Smuggler negotiated the distance in 2:15¼, and in the best of sports-writing jargon the local press proclaimed that "there never was a more exciting contest."[22] Smuggler was a western import foaled in Ohio in 1866 and trained in Leavenworth, Kansas, by W. E. Tough. He was brought to New England by Colonel H. S. Russell of Milton, Massachusetts. Russell—the owner of another superb stallion, Fearnaught—bought Smuggler for a price in excess of $30,000. Smuggler's natural gait had been the pace, and to keep him to the trot he carried 24 ounces of lead on his forefeet.[23]

The best trotters of the day toured the Middle West as well as the East. For example, Judge Fullerton trotted against Goldsmith Maid at East Saginaw, Michigan, on July 18, 1874. Even in a colored lithograph there is the feeling of a thousand hushed voices and breathless silence in the instant or two that the panting steeds flew down the track toward the judges' stand. The tenseness was broken only by the harsh voices of the two drivers and the crack of their whips. The print depicting this event, an undated colored lithograph, captures the excitement shared at the East Saginaw Driving Park by the eight thousand

21. Ibid. See also *The Boston Daily Globe*, September 16, 1874.   22. *The Hartford Daily Courant*, September 1, 1876.   23. Walter T. Chester, compil., *Chester's Complete Trotting and Pacing Record* (New York, 1884), p. 809; Wallace, *Horse of America*, pp. 357–358.

2:19¾
2:16½
2:16

Judge Fullerton   Goldsmith Maid

BEST TIME ON RECORD. THREE HEATS IN 2:19¾ 2:16½ 2:16.

Goldsmith Maid and Judge Fullerton, in their great trot at east saginaw, mich. July 16th 1874.

Purse, $5000 $2500 to first, $1500 to second, and $1000 to the horse which deats 2:16¾ mile heats, 3 in 5 in harness

Budd Doble's b.m. Goldsmith Maid 1.1.1. B. Mace's ch g. Judge Fullerton 2.2.2.

persons who saw "the fastest three heats ever made." Crowds at trotting events in the 1870s were both knowing and dedicated, or at least they were in Michigan. When, in the last heat, the Maid came across the line in 2:16 flat, "there was a universal uprising on the grandstand . . . [and] the ladies seemed more enthusiastic than the men." One gentleman upon turning around "saw a woman near him waving her handkerchief with all her might, but upon looking down he saw her baby lying at her feet and beginning to cry. 'Madam,' said he, 'Your child,' pointing to it. 'Oh' said she 'I forgot all about baby: but it makes no difference; I expect to have several babies, but I never expect to see another Goldsmith Maid!' "[24]

East Saginaw had one of the newest and most accurately laid trotting courses in the country, and on it the amazing Goldsmith Maid, in her seventeenth year, continued to reign—following Lady Suffolk and Flora Temple—as Queen of the Turf. The Maid was foaled in 1857 and carried the blood of the Abdallah strain on both sides. She was a blood bay, and, through 1870, she had won over $58,000. Judge Fullerton was a chestnut gelding with one of the most impressive trotting records on the circuit in the 1870s. (The white-stockinged, blaze-faced horse in the print is Judge Fullerton and not Goldsmith Maid as captioned.) The drivers in this race at East Saginaw were Budd Doble driving the Maid and Dan Mace handling the reins of the Judge. This print is an anonymous issue of "The Best Time On Record." It appears to be a version of the Currier & Ives print of the same title copyrighted in 1874. In the Peters print the positions of the horses have been reversed, and the titles left the same. The Currier & Ives folio includes only part of the judges' stand, which in this version of the print is shown in its entirety.[25]

The popularity of the trotting horse appealed to commercial interests, and many used

24. *The Detroit Free Press*, July 17, 1874; *Jackson Daily Citizen*, July 20, 1874.   25. *Frank Forester*, vol. 2, p. 250.

track champions in their advertising. Donaldson Brothers, of Five Points, New York, produced a colored lithograph for the Vacuum Oil Company of Rochester in 1874 that featured Goldsmith Maid. The handsome print is a lovely soft-sell visual for the oil company, and it makes good use of two of Goldsmith Maid's finest track performances—one at Rochester in August and the other at Mystic Park in September 1874. Goldsmith Maid, in topping Dexter's mark in 1871, became the top trotting horse in America, a position she held for eight years. During this period she reduced the record time for the mile from 2:17 to 2:14, which she trotted at Mystic Park in September 1874. Her record stood until 1878 when Rarus covered the distance in 2:13¼. The folio advertisement by John Cameron, an artist usually associated with Currier & Ives' horse prints, documents the Maid's greatest year in harness. The finish line at Rochester's Driving Park is the scene, and it includes, along with Budd Doble and Goldsmith Maid, the judges' stand, filled on this day in August with celebrities (including William Vanderbilt). The judges, with a crowd of 25,000 eager fans looking on, called for the "Free For All." This was the big race of the day, and it pitted the Maid against American Girl and Judge Fullerton. The Maid won all three heats on a wet track—the second in the splendid time of 2:14¾—and to a man all agreed that they had seen "a good, square, honest piece of magnificent trotting."[26] Three weeks later at Mystic Park the Maid went again, not against competition but against the clock, under what were described as "the most favorable auspices."[27] There was absolutely no wind at the time of the race. The track had been prepared beautifully by scraping it very close into the pole, and, amidst all this, the fall meeting at Mystic was being chided in the press as a "trotting carnival." On the day of the race, in spite of the dust, dirt, and delays, "everybody was there, from the common betting man, with dingy felt hat and profusion of jewelry, to the staid merchant, who looked somewhat ill at ease in the throng of anxious turfmen." They

26. *Rochester Daily Union and Advertiser*, August 13, 1874.   27. *The New York Times*, September 3, 1874.

THE CELEBRATED
VACUUM OIL BLACKING
Fits Harness Perfectly

AUGUST 12TH 1874 · 2.14¾ · AT ROCHESTER, N.Y. GOLDSMITH MAID. SEPT. 2ND 1874 · 2.14 · AT MYSTIC PARK

Published by Vacuum Oil Co. Rochester N.Y.

all had come to see the "Queen of the Turf," and when she and her driver, Budd Doble, appeared they were "most heartily cheered by the crowd." As was the custom, the Maid took a turn around the track, and it was the consensus of those along the rail that she resembled "well the pictures which have been made of her." The bold type of the morning paper in Boston—"TWO-FOURTEEN!"—told the story of the trot.[28]

The horse prints of Haskell & Allen were, according to Harry T. Peters, "their most memorable products," although in the number produced they ran a poor second by comparison to the output of Currier & Ives.[29] Two which survive in the Peters Collection are typical of lithographs published because of local interest and appeal. Ben Morrill enjoyed no special distinction except that of being a local Boston favorite. The big brown stallion appeared frequently between 1872 and 1878 throughout New England and Canada.[30] On the day depicted in the print, Ben, driven by J. J. Bowen, won two of nine heats at Prospect Park Fair Grounds in a special race for trotters who had never been under the time of 2:30 for the mile. In this race, however, Ben Morrill neither won the purse nor had the best time. Ben Morrill was not the caliber of most of the Grand Circuit trotters portrayed by the nineteenth-century printmakers. Another Boston favorite was Smuggler, and those who trotted against him (for example, Great Eastern from New York) always commanded a good press and, not infrequently, good lithographic coverage as well. To look at the Haskell & Allen print of Great Eastern as he appeared at Mystic Park in 1876, one would never guess that "it was an uncomfortable day, the wind blowing so hard as to discourage very many and destroy the pleasure of the rest." Nevertheless, over 3000 persons braved the elements to see what they thought would be an easy win for the local hero, Smuggler, over the brown gelding from New York. True to form, Smuggler won the first heat easily, although in the second he made several breaks and was easily distanced. After this heat the

28. *The Boston Daily Globe,* September 3, 1874. 29. Peters, *America on Stone,* p. 206. 30. *The New York Times,* October 31, 1874; *Chester's Complete Trotting Record,* p. 54.

BEN MORRILL,

OWNED BY T.B. WILLIAMS (BOSTON, MASS.) GOT BY WINTHROP MORRILL, DAM BY OLD COLUMBUS.

Won a number of Trots in 1874 and trotted at Prospect Park, Oct. 29th 1874.

BEST TIME 2:28.

From the Original Painting by Scott Leighton.

GREAT EASTERN,

AS HE APPEARED IN THE TRIO RACES WITH SMUGGLER AT MYSTIC PARK, BOSTON, OCT. 10. 1876,

when the latter was distanced in first race, and beaten in the second

TIME 2:21, 2:21½, 2:23.

RARUS,

THE FASTEST TROTTING HORSE IN THE WORLD.

Best Time 2.13¼.

judges announced that the horses would meet again on October 20th. It was on this date, not the 16th, that Great Eastern beat Smuggler in the times recorded on the Haskell & Allen print. In his several outings against Smuggler at Mystic Park, Great Eastern was driven by A. J. Feek. Between 1875 and 1883 he was a winner thirteen times in events that took him as far west as Illinois.[31]

If Great Eastern as a performer was not up to the usual quality of horses enshrined by printmakers, Rarus was. Any doubt was surely dispelled in 1878 by F. M. Haskell & Co., of Boston, whose print of Rarus carried the subcaption, "The Fastest Trotting Horse in the World." For a brief time Rarus was King of the Turf. On August 3, 1878, at Buffalo, he had beaten Goldsmith Maid's record for the mile in what was headlined as "The Greatest Achievement on Record." The day had been perfect and the crowd large, and, as for Rarus, he had been "full of life and his eyes sparkled with intelligence." Keen observers noted too that his ears "were constantly moving backward and forward, as though he was trying to hear what was said." (The Haskell print gives precisely this impression.) Rarus's driver for this assault on time was John Splan of Cleveland, "well-known and skillful." At about 2:45 in the afternoon after several bad starts, the attempt on the record began. Rarus was to trot against the clock, and when he finally got away he did so "at a terrific pace, his speed being seen to the best advantage at the turn." He reached the quarter-mile post without the sign of a break in 33½ seconds, and in the back stretch he increased his speed, passing the half-mile pole in 1:5¾. This was an astonishing time for a trotting horse. He lapsed momentarily just beyond the half-mile pole, but this was barely noticeable from the stands. Past the three-quarter pole he sped in 1:38½, and, noting this, it was now perfectly obvious to the faithful in the stands that this would be a day to remember—provided, of course, that Rarus did not break. The excitement increased, and every-

---

31. *Boston Daily Advertiser*, October 17, 1876; *Chester's Complete Trotting Record*, p. 281.

one watched with the keenest interest as the spirited horse neared the finish. Splan applied his whip for the first time when he was almost home. Under the wire flew Rarus, and the timers marked "Two Minutes and Thirteen And One Quarter Seconds." It was a record unparalleled. Rarus was a Long Island horse owned by R. B. Concklin. He was of the Abdallah strain and had made his first trot in 1874. At the time of the record trot he was well known for a series of races against Goldsmith Maid both on the East and West coasts. Rarus's record, however, was short lived in a decade of speedsters. In the very next season, 1879, St. Julien made the mile in 2:12¾, followed in 1880 by Maud S with 2:10¾, a mark she subsequently reduced to 2:08¾ in 1885.[32] After Buffalo, Rarus was promptly purchased by Robert Bonner. He joined Dexter and other famous trotters on Bonner's farm in Tarrytown, where between 1860 and 1890 the publisher of the *New York Ledger* managed to house most of the great champions of the turf.

The last trotter-to-sulky print in the Peters Collection is a view of Jay Eye See, once again an advertisement for the Vacuum Oil Company of Rochester. The print is a black-and-white photo-oleograph and was published in 1884. Jay Eye See's "well-knit frame and small but firmly moulded legs" are nicely drawn. The excitement of the day and the thrill engendered by the performance of a first-rate animal are clearly carried in the print, and it makes an effective advertisement as well as a pleasing lithograph. There was complete agreement on this early fall day in Providence that the horse was a splendid sight as "the sun's rays glistened on his glossy jet-black coat." He held his head high, and his "clear, dark eyes surveyed with evident interest the crowd of expectant watchers." His action was perfect as he got away from the start, with never the suspicion of a skip or a break. Moving easily and gracefully with a swinging stride, he made the quarter post in 34 seconds. Some in the stands felt he would not make his mark, but, as Jay Eye See moved into the straight-

---

32. *Commercial Advertiser* (Buffalo), August 5, 1878; *American Agriculturist*, vol. 42 (August 1883), p. 355.

PHOTO-OLEOGRAPH BY CLAY & RICHMOND, BUFFALO, N.Y.

COPYRIGHTED 1884 BY CLAY & RICHMOND, BUFFALO, N.Y.

BEST TIME
2.10¾ AT PROVIDENCE, R.I.
SEPT. 15TH 1883

JAY EYE SEE.

PUBLISHED BY
VACUUM OIL COMPANY
ROCHESTER, N.Y.

away on the backstretch, his pace grew faster and faster. Still there was no suggestion of a flaw in his splendid motion. He passed the three-quarter post in 1:30, and the people were now on their feet, shouting, "He's got it, He's got it." Watches were checked, and the noise mounted. The jockey, Ned Bithers, urged Jay Eye See gently. He swung his whip but did not strike the horse. He did not need to—a final stride and Jay Eye See was under the wire. The race was over. There was a momentary hush, and the judge announced the time: 2:10¾. For a brief but exciting instant in the annals of American trotting-horse history, this five-year-old black gelding, Jay Eye See, was undoubtedly, as once were his record-breaking predecessors, "the greatest wonder now on the turf." Not since Flora Temple in her halcyon days had Narragansett Park been in such a furor. The five thousand spectators had witnessed "A Great Trotting Event" on the Grand Circuit.[33] Although Currier & Ives' trotting gallery is more extensive and more complete, the random prints in the Peters Collection by lithographers in various eastern cities have captured the true spirit of the sulky race.

33. *The Providence Journal*, September 17, 1883.

The pragmatic relationship between sport and pleasure in nineteenth-century America is personified by the trotter-to-wagon contests witnessed at trotting tracks in the middle decades of the century. The nine prints illustrating wagon races in the Peters Collection suggest roughly the proportionate frequency of their occurrence as compared to saddle and in-harness matches. Generally, if the print is an index, the trotting fraternity progressed from saddle to sulky, to wagon for a time, and (by the 1870s on the Grand Circuit) back to the almost exclusive use of the sulky. Improved roads, light, strong vehicles, and excellent, simply designed harness all favored speed on the road. The fast times on the trotting track stimulated an increase on the road, and after 1860 there was a perceptible gain in speed capability in the general level of trotting stock throughout the country.

The Thomas & Eno print, "The Greatest Performance in Double Harness on Record," was a model of attainment for drivers in all circumstances.[1] In it are Lady Palmer and the Flatbush Mare, beautifully turned out and driven by their owner, Robert Bonner. In May of 1862 Bonner completed against time a 2:12 mile with this outstanding pair hitched to a road wagon. There was no greater exponent of fast wagon driving than Robert Bonner, the simon-pure publisher of the *New York Ledger*. He condemned the practice of betting as an evil and devoted a lifetime to improving the harness horse, enjoying the pleasures of the road, and protesting the over-commercialization of this American pastime. The colored lithograph by Thomas & Eno preserves a visual record of one of Bonner's memorable feats, an effort over the Fashion Course on Long Island to prove beyond question to Commodore Vanderbilt that the "*Ledger* team was without peer." Bonner felt that his superb team, perfectly matched and "of the finest mould, full of life, and elastic vigor," was unbeatable.

1. See "Among the Blue-Grass Trotters," *Harper's New Monthly Magazine*, vol. 67, pp. 727–728. The writer thought that, despite the elegance displayed in lithographs of Bonner and Grant, seen hanging on "every horse-fancier's wall in the country," it was the trotter himself, "like a piece of our light and elegant machinery," that should always be the center of attraction and praise. When this was not the case, it indicated an artist's failure.

THOMAS & ENO. LITH. 37 PARK ROW, N.Y.

THE GREATEST PERFORMANCE IN DOUBLE HARNESS ON RECORD—A 2:12 GAIT TO A ROAD WAGON.

Lady Palmer and Flatbush Mare, driven by their Owner, Mr. Bonner.—taken out of his Stable, untrained.—to a Road Wagon in Public.—

May 10, 1862.—ONE MILE in 2:26. May 13, 1862.—TWO MILES in 5:01¼—the SECOND QUARTER of the SECOND MILE in 33 SECONDS, being a 2:12 gait to a Road Wagon.

With Bonner driving and Vanderbilt holding the watch, the matched pair trotted the two miles in 5:01¼, moving through the second mile "with the steadiness of a locomotive." This event focused public attention on the driving of trotting horses more clearly than any other single match in the history of trotting competition. Bonner, elated by the accomplishment of his team, in lieu of a bet offered $10,000 to anyone posting a better time. The print is based on a painting by Theodore Marsden as engraved by W. G. Jackson for Forester's *Horse and Horsemanship of the United States.* In every detail the print captures the spirit and elegance of proper driving.[2]

A high degree of artistic license is apparent in the popular lithograph, and to printmakers' eyes all races were close. In a memorable meeting on Long Island between Dexter and General Butler on October 27, 1865, Dexter took both heats by better than two lengths. Nonetheless, artists who recorded this important race invariably showed Dexter the winner by only a head. General Butler, prior to his meeting with Dexter, had the fastest time thus far recorded by a trotter over the distance of two miles hitched to wagon. Dexter, on the other hand, had seldom competed harnessed to a wagon, and anticipation of this match had "created unusual excitement in the trotting world."[3] The condition of the principals on race day matched all expectations. Dexter, as his driver Hiram Woodruff matter-of-factly related, was at his peak, the perfection of trotting. He was calm despite the newness of the wagon style, and during the race itself he never made a break. His speed was constant and well distributed over the distance. The Peters print of this event, though undated, is apparently a folio of a smaller print by Currier & Ives issued in 1874 which

2. Robert McClure, ed., *Every Horse Owners' Cyclopedia* (Philadelphia, 1872), pp. 542–543. The trotting horse was so popular and the endorsement he received from such notables as Grant, Bonner, Vanderbilt, et al., so well publicized that *Harper's New Monthly*, vol. 67, p. 722, could write that the trotter was "recognized as so essentially American a product that he might almost be engraved on the national shield." 3. *The New York Times,* October 28, 1865. Even the best horses, when harnessed to wagons, were six seconds slower as a rule than trotters harnessed to sulky. See McClure, ed., *Every Horse Owners' Cyclopedia*, p. 538 fn.

bears the same title and is after a drawing by J. Cameron. In the Peters print, however, Dexter is incorrectly listed as a winner of three heats over Butler, when the race in question was for only two. The match between Dexter and General Butler is the subject of another print in the Peters Collection. In this version, an undated colored lithograph, only Dexter is shown, having presumably outdistanced Butler by two lengths as he moved along the backstretch by the stands. The driver, as shown in the print, is Hiram Woodruff.[4]

In 1867 Thomas Kelly of New York published a colored lithograph of Dexter "as he appeared" at the Fashion Course on June 21, 1867, the day of his big race against Ethan Allen. The print erroneously shows Dexter hitched to a wagon. Actually, he had trotted in harness against Ethan and his running mate, as correctly shown in the Haskell print of this race. The Kelly print is grossly executed and caricatures the previously mentioned anonymous print proclaiming Dexter's wagon victory over General Butler; its caption records Dexter's losing time against Ethan and his mate. The stiff and unlifelike driver portrayed is intended as Hiram Woodruff. Presumably he was so well known that even this poor rendering was to be immediately recognized. So unimportant were details in a poor-quality, low-priced print that the caption might describe Dexter as a brown horse and the artist actually render him (as did Kelly) as a black.[5]

Ethan Allen, a colored lithograph published in 1868 by C. H. Crosby, of Boston, from Marsden's *American Horses*, is a splendid print by contrast, with details of horse, wagon, and driver carefully drawn and with composition and typography pristine. Again, the scene may be imagined as the backstretch of Fashion Course, Long Island, on June 21, 1867, and the match depicted is Ethan Allen's victory over Dexter. Instead of showing the winning team, the print shows only Ethan going at full clip hitched to a road wagon. His

4. Hiram Woodruff, *The Trotting Horse of America* (New York, 1868), pp. 362–366.   5. Ibid., pp. 407–408; *The New York Times*, June 23, 1867.

GENERAL BUTLER AND DEXTER.

Match for $ 2,000, two Mile heats, to Wagons, over the Fashion Course, L. I. Oct! 27th 1865.

H. Woodruff's Br. G. Dexter 1.1.1. D. Tallman's Bl. G. General Butler 2.2.2.

Time,   5:00¾,   4:56¼.

FASHION COURSE, L. I. OCT 10TH 1865.
E. V. W. SNEDEKER WAGERED $5000 TO 1000, THAT THE HORSE DEXTER
(TROTTING I MILE) COULD NOT BEAT 2 MIN. 19 SEC. H. WOODRUFF ENTERED BR.
HORSE DEXTER, RIDDEN BY JOHN MURPHY, 145 LBS. WON.___TIME, 2: 18½
FASHION COURSE, L.I. OCT. 27TH 1865. MATCH $2000, 2 MILE HEATS TO WAGON,

H. WOODRUFF'S BR. G. DEXTER,	1	1
H. TALLMAN'S, BLK G. GEN. BUTLER,	2	2
	Time, 5:00¾ 4:56¼	

DEXTER,
THE RENOWNED HORSE DEXTER, AS HE APPEARED ON FASHION COURSE, L.I. DRIVEN BY HIRAM WOODRUFF.

DEXTER, IS A BROWN GELDING 15 HANDS 1 INCH HIGH, FOALED IN 1858. SIRED
BY RYSDYK'S HAMBLETONIAN, DAM HAWKINS MARE BY AMERICAN STAR
HE WAS RAISED BY JONATHAN HAWKINS, MONTGOMERY, ORANGE C? N.Y.
AVON SPRINGS, N. Y. HALF MILE TRACK, AUG. 6TH 1866, PURSE $ 1000 MILE HEATS
IN HARNESS.

B. DOBLE'S BR. G. DEXTER,	1	1
J. I. EOFF'S BS. GEO. M PATCHEN,	2	2
	Time, 2 31½ 2:21	

Publ. & Print. by Th. Kelly.

Entered according to act of Congress in the year 1867 by Th. Kelly in the Office of the Librarian of Congress at Washington D.C.

17 Barclay St. N.Y.

DEXTER is a brown gelding 15 hands 1 inch high   **DEXTER,**   Dam Hawkins Mare by AMERICAN STAR he was raised
foaled in 1858 sired by Rysdyk's HAMBLETONIAN   by Jonathan Hawkins Montgomery Orange Cº N.Y.

The renowned horse DEXTER as he appeared on Fashion Course L.I. driven by Hiram Woodruff
DEXTER'S fastest time 2 16¾ on Fashion Course June 21ˢᵗ 1867.

C. H. Crosby Lith.

Entered according to Act of Congress, in the year 1866 by T. Marsden, in the Clerk's Office of the District Court for the District of Massachusetts.

ETHAN ALLEN.

The Property of S. E. Maynard Esq.   Time: 2.15 — 2.16 — 2.19.

ETHAN ALLEN

owner, J. E. Maynard, is driving. The Marsden portrait technically might be classified a road scene; it is captioned, however, with Ethan's winning time in one of the great trotting matches of the decade and is thus pertinent in the present context. In contrast to this really superb print is another to-wagon print in the Peters Collection by Haskell & Allen, once again of Ethan Allen. Here Ethan is shown correctly as a bright bay, with his most distinguishing characteristic a sweeping, waving tail, which, as Frank Forester confided, the animal "actually trod upon . . . more than once"—a considerable change since the days of dock-tailed trotters like Whalebone and Columbus.[6] The variation in quality of these several prints of Dexter and Ethan Allen indicates the wide range of choice available to print buyers as well as the wide range of taste and knowledge to which the printmakers catered.

Printmakers existed by pleasing a demanding public, and frequently they took considerable liberty in the presentation of fact and reality. George Kelly's print which purportedly shows Dexter Park in Chicago, where in 1867 General Butler, Silas Rich, and Bashaw Jr. trotted for a purse of $2800, is a good example of the broad liberties permissible in an age untuned to factual pictorial reporting. To an uncritical public seeing only this print it appeared that Silas Rich had beaten General Butler and Bashaw Jr. in a tight and exciting trotting match. Actually, none of these trotters won on this particular Thursday in Chicago—Silas Rich finished second, Bashaw Jr., third, and General Butler, last! All were behind the winner, none other than Dexter, who made the time shown correctly on the Kelly print. Carrying inaccuracy even further, the stalwarts pictured by Kelly competed in harness, not to-wagon, against Dexter, who actually went to the pole hitched to a wagon! This print should be closely compared to the following one, also by Kelly, which

6. For C. H. Crosby and also Marsden, see Harry T. Peters, *America on Stone* (Garden City, N.Y., 1931), pp. 148–149, 272. Henry William Herbert [Frank Forester], *The Horse and Horsemanship of the United States and the British Provinces of North America* (New York, 1871), vol. 2, p. 105 (hereafter cited *Frank Forester*), states that another splendid horse portraitist, William Attwood, actually saw Ethan do this while being painted.

shows Lady Thorne and American Girl. Note that in the two views the tracks, one in Chicago and one on Long Island, are for all purposes identical. Also, note that, except for coloring, the position, stance, and gait of General Butler and Silas Rich are precisely the same as those of Lady Thorne and American Girl. By changing the facial expressions of the drivers on the Lady Thorne version, the publisher illustrated two events widely separated in space and time. He simply altered his stone, a fact apparent from the remnant of the wagon wheel still visible on the Lady Thorne print. The niceties of accurate delineation and presentation were not allowed to interfere with the economics of printmaking. Nevertheless, the two Kelly prints are particularly handsome examples of the lithographer's art, if not his veracity. (Of the horses depicted in this race at Chicago, Bashaw Jr. needs a word of introduction. He was a dark-chestnut stallion of substantial size, particularly well-known in the Middle West, and many trackmen of the late 1860s considered him the "best of any horse west of the Allegheny Mountains." It is likely also that he was the best of the Bashaw strain, whose chief progenitor had been Grand Bashaw, imported from Tripoli to Philadelphia by the American consul, Richard Jones, in 1820; Grand Bashaw had stood stud through the year 1845 in Lower Merion in Montgomery County, Pennsylvania.[7])

In the year 1869 Dexter was retired, and Goldsmith Maid had yet to show her best. For one trotting season at least Lady Thorne and American Girl were "confessedly, the fastest horses now on the American trotting turf."[8] The announcement of a head-to-head meeting of this pair had engendered great interest, and the pre-race enthusiasm had drawn over twelve thousand persons to the track on a Monday afternoon. The Fashion Course had not been so crowded since the great race between Dexter and Ethan Allen and his mate. Lady Thorne earlier in the year had beaten American Girl not once but several times. Her win-

7. See the *Chicago Tribune*, September 6, 1867. For Bashaw Jr., see Hamilton Busbey, "The Trotting Horse in America," *Harper's New Monthly Magazine*, vol. 47, p. 606; Woodruff, *Trotting Horse*, p. 76; and *Frank Forester*, vol. 2, p. 273.   8. *The New York Times*, July 13, 1869.

Pbd by Geo. Kelly

Entered according to act of Congress AD 1867 by Geo. Kelly in the Clerks Office of the District Court of the So. D. District of Penn.

GEN. BUTLER, SILUS RICH & BASHAW Jr.

Trotting for a Purse of $2,800, or Handecaps 3 in 5 Mile Heats, at Dexter Park, Chicago, Ill. Sept 5th 1867

TIME 2.30½, 2.28½, 2.30½

Publ. by Geo. Kelly

Entered according to act of Congress A.D.1869 by Geo.Kelly in the Clerk's Office of the District Court of the East". District of Penn."

LADY THORN AND AMERICAN GIRL
IN THEIR GREAT MATCH FOR $ 2'500 MILE HEATS BEST 3 in 5 to WAGONS.
OVER THE FASHION COURSE. L. I. JULY 12th 1869.

| M.RODEN B.M. AMERICAN GIRL | 1 1 2 1 |
| B. PFIFERS B.M. LADY THORN | 2 2 1 1 |

Time, 2'28⅗. 2'24¾. 2'27¾. 2'24½.

ning margins had been close, and at least once so close that the judges' call was questionable. This race would settle once and for all which of the two bay mares was the faster, and to assure an all-out effort the track management at Fashion Course offered a purse of $2500. The race was in harness, not to-wagon as Kelly's print erroneously illustrates. In the race itself American Girl took the first heat by three quarters of a length and the second by a short neck, lost the third by a similar margin, and took the fourth by a good half length. The print captions incorrectly list the Lady and the Girl both as winners of the fourth heat![9] Though handsome, the two Kelly prints are most inaccurate representations of the races and the animals they portrayed to the sporting public. Only to experts or to persons who had carefully observed Lady Thorne, however, would it have mattered that the mare, contrary to her likeness in the print, had no white on her at all or that in a series of Kelly lithographs a single horse portrait passed for whomever the caption called for. Thus, General Butler easily became Lady Thorne, and vice versa. Trotting enthusiasts wanted to read news of the track; they also wanted illustrations of the big events of the day and the participants in them. The print provided both, and who was to know, or indeed care, that frequently the details depicted did not fit the facts? Lady Thorne, despite her loss to American Girl, was one of trotting history's great mares. Big, powerful, and with amazing endurance, she had been foaled in Kentucky in 1856, sired by Mambrino Chief. Dan Pfifer was her driver and trainer throughout most of her career, and together they lost few big races.[10] As is often the case in the history of American sport, the defeat of a champion by an underdog is an event of considerable popular moment. The afternoon on which American Girl mastered Lady Thorne was such a day.

Not all track prints were inaccurate, and indeed, although it may seem so, not all to-wagon prints were poor. Mayer & Merkel, of New York, printed a colored lithograph in

9. Ibid.   10. Busbey, "Trotting Horse," *Harper's New Monthly*, vol. 47, pp. 609, 611. See also *Frank Forester,* vol. 2, pp. 240, 244.

1869 of Volunteer which is a decided contrast to Kelly's views of General Butler, Bashaw, American Girl, and Lady Thorne. There is a sense of reality in this long-striding interpretation of Volunteer which places the viewer in the seat and the reins in his hands. It is this quality perhaps that makes it today "a very scarce trotting print."[11] The faithfulness of the print was undoubtedly owing in part to the fact that Alden Goldsmith, Volunteer's owner, held the copyright. The widely distributed picture of the horse and owner presumably increased the patronage of the stallion. Volunteer was foaled in 1854 in Orange County, New York. He was the son of the most productive and illustrious sire of trotting stock in the nineteenth century, Rysdyk's Hambletonian, and he was judged by contemporary connoisseurs of the horse Hambletonian's most handsome heir. Volunteer was a bay, and, as shown correctly in the print, he had just a bit of white around his left coronet. Most descriptions cite his elegance of carriage; the print stresses this quality by accentuating his lofty head and graceful neck. Alden Goldsmith, owner of the remarkable mare, Goldsmith Maid, purchased Volunteer in 1861. Prior to Goldsmith's purchase, the horse had been called Hambletonian Jr., but—with patriotic sentiment high—his name was changed. Volunteer's reputation as a progenitor of first-rate trotters began about 1871. Among the portraits in the Peters Collection is one of Volunteer's son, St. Julien, who at 2:11¼ was for a time the fastest trotter in the world. Volunteer died in 1888 at the extraordinary age of 34. As a sire he had contributed mightily to the perfection of the standardbred horse. The traits with which Victorian Americans felt themselves to be endowed were transferred easily to this improved breed of animal. "Volunteer," it was said, "stands pre-eminent among trotting sires as the one horse against not one of whose get the epithet 'quitter' was . . . ever hurled."[12] High praise indeed for horse or man, and Volunteer measured up to the mark.

11. Peters, *America on Stone,* p. 277.   12. John H. Wallace, *Horse of America* (New York, 1897), p. 301.

Trotters to Wagon

The to-wagon prints as a group tend to be less appealing, less accurate, and of lesser quality than the other groups of trotting prints in the Peters Collection. The explanation seems to lie in the fact that this form of the sport was irregularly scheduled and short-lived and thus not as well understood by artists and lithographers. The delineation of a trotter under saddle or hitched to a sulky was usually detailed and convincing. Although wagons on the road were acceptably drawn, the idea of the light racing road wagon on the track and the excitement it surely caused was never quite captured on the lithographer's stone.

"All artists," wrote J. D. B. Stillman in his discussion of Muybridge's photographic studies, "know the value of the horse as a *chef d'oeuvre*, and he is made, next to the human figure, the first subject in elementary studies in art." That the lithographic artist was no exception is largely verified by Harry Peters' opinion that portraits of trotters alone constituted the third-largest subject-matter group to be put on stone.[1] Horse portraits by American lithographers are generally either illustrations originally intended for periodicals and books; advertisements prepared for wagon builders and dealers in horse furnishings; prints attesting (in a slightly more attractive manner than the broadside) the powers of a stud or the speed of a champion trotter; or likenesses—based on paintings—of famous animals owned by illustrious horsemen of the period. Only passing reference has been made thus far to Flora Temple, a trotting champion almost without peer in mid-nineteenth-century America. Interestingly, for this mare was a marvel in motion, she is not portrayed in action in any of the four prints preserved in the Peters Collection. In these she is seen either standing quietly in her stall or bucolically posed in a gently rolling meadow. Only in the captions of these serene and pastoral portraits are the dates and times of her great days on the track found.

On September 2, 1856, at the Union Course, Long Island, Flora Temple trotted the mile in 2:24½ in harness. Porter's *Spirit of the Times*, a weekly journal conceived by William T. Porter in the 1830s and devoted to horses, racing, hunting, fishing, and gaming of all sorts, celebrated the event by issuing a colored wood engraving. Porter's periodical was the first regularly published sporting journal in the United States. In 1856, about the time that this print of Flora was published, George Wilkes acquired control of Porter's journal.

1. J. D. B. Stillman, *The Horse in Motion* (Boston, 1882), p. 101. Leland Stanford had employed Muybridge and Stillman to make this study. Harry T. Peters, *America on Stone* (Garden City, N.Y., 1931), p. 180. The prototype of American trotting prints was published in England early in the 19th century. For an interesting comparison, see R. S. Summerhays, "Oldtime Trotter into Modern Hackney," in *Country Life* (July 15, 1965), pp. 162–163.

FLORA TEMPLE.

2:24½ in harness, Union Course L.I. Sept 2. 1856.

Lith. and pub. by Spirit of the Times

H 86

Wilkes' relationship with Porter continued until 1859, when he began his own sporting newspaper, which he called *Wilkes' Spirit of the Times*. It was Wilkes' good fortune to have retained Charles Foster as a feature writer. Porter continued in competition with Wilkes until the early 1860s, then discontinued publication.[2]

Flora's victory on the Union Course in 1856 was "the fastest heat ever trotted" there up to that time.[3] In this race she had beaten the Canadian-bred Tacony, who had gone to the post under saddle. Later the same year at Kalamazoo, Flora lowered the mark to a spectacular 2:19¾, a time not bettered by a trotter until Dexter came along almost a decade later. Flora Temple followed Lady Suffolk as the country's most famous trotting mare. She was foaled in 1845 near Utica, New York, and died in 1877. To Hiram Woodruff she epitomized the "three prime qualities in the trotting horse; viz., speed, bottom, and the power to pull weight." To Frank Forester the diminutive bay mare was "a little treasure in action." To George Wilkes, the publicist, who endowed her with a voice, she was "little as I am . . . mistress of the trotting-turf." The press which reported her exploits in 1856 generally agreed that "since the days of Lady Suffolk no nag has stood higher in the estimation of sporting men than Flora Temple."[4]

In 1859 a lithograph was published of Flora Temple after a portrait by William F. Attwood. In addition to this sensitive rendering of Flora, Attwood did accurate portraits of Ethan Allen and Black Hawk, both of which appeared as engravings in Forester's *Horse and Horsemanship of the United States* (1857). Attwood exhibited at the National Acad-

---

2. John H. Wallace, *The Horse of America* (New York, 1897), pp. 98–99. 3. *New York Daily Times*, September 3, 1856. 4. For a succinct statement of Flora's best times, see Hamilton Busbey, "The Trotting Horse in America," *Harper's New Monthly Magazine*, vol. 47, pp. 607–608; and Robert McClure, ed., *Every Horse Owner's Cyclopedia* (Philadelphia, 1872), pp. 537–540. Flora's qualities as a trotter are found in Hiram Woodruff, *The Trotting Horse of America* (New York, 1868), pp. 256, 258; and Henry William Herbert [Frank Forester], *Frank Forester's Horse and Horsemanship of the United States and the British Provinces of North America* (New York, 1871), vol. 2, pp. 234, 238.

FLORA TEMPLE.

The Property of Wm. McDonald Esq, Baltimore.

Photographed by Fredericks from the Original Painting by W.F. Atwood in possession of W.McDonald Esq.

emy and worked mostly in and around New York. Apparently he also had Baltimore patronage since, in addition to the Flora Temple done for William Macdonald, he did a portrait of Mr. and Mrs. George S. Brown driving a tandem rig near their Baltimore estate. Macdonald, credited in the print's caption as owner both of the Attwood portrait and of Flora, had purchased the horse in 1858 for $8000. This print is of particular interest because it is based on a photograph of the Attwood painting taken by Charles D. Fredricks, Matthew Brady's most formidable competitor. Fredricks was proprietor of a gallery studio which some contemporary opinion held to be more elegant than any salon in Paris or in London.[5]

The third print portrait of Flora in the Peters Collection is one published by John Smith of Philadelphia in 1869 entitled "The Celebrated American Trotting Mare." Flora Temple's fifteen years in harness made her a favorite of the printmakers and her exploits were largely responsible for the first burst of public enthusiasm for trotting meets. By 1861 nearly every town of over three thousand inhabitants supported a trotting track, and Flora had become a symbol. For a generation she personified speed, improved horseflesh, and the excitement of newfound leisure time. Flora was acquired by George Welch of Chestnut Hill in 1860, and during her lifetime the price paid for fine trotting stock commonly ranged between $10,000 and $20,000. The print shows Flora with a colt.

The last portrait of Flora Temple is a colored lithograph, dated 1869 and published by Bradley & Company from a painting by James Queen after E. Troye. The print is not captioned, but the cropped tail, the bay color, the dark legs, mane, and tail unquestionably belong to Flora. The print by Queen (after Troye) combines the techniques of two of the more skilled horse painters of the period. Individually their efforts brought considerable

5. Geoge C. Groce and David H. Wallace, *New-York Historical Society's Dictionary of Artists in America 1564–1860* (New Haven, 1957), p. 15; see also John Wege, *The Evolution of Photography* (London, 1890), p. 72, and Robert Taft, *Photography and the American Scene* (New York, 1938), p. 196.

PUB. BY JOHN SMITH, 210 RANSOM ST. PHILAD.

THE CELEBRATED AMERICAN TROTTING MARE,

FLORA TEMPLE AND COLT.

NOW OWNED BY

GEORGE WELCH,

CHESTNUT HILL, O.

Untitled [Flora Temple and Colt].

quality and accuracy to this phase of popular art. Troye's best known work was a fine portrait of the running horse, Black Maria, painted in 1834 which, astonishingly, shows this famous and valuable animal carelessly and unceremoniously hitched to a tree.[6]

Sarony, Major & Knapp, of New York, in 1860 put on stone a composite portrait entitled "Trotting Gallery" adapted from a painting by W. F. Attwood. "Trotting Gallery" is another delightful piece of mid-nineteenth-century advertising matter published by one of the best known American carriage builders, Brewster & Co. In 1810 the Brewsters had begun business in New Haven, moving subsequently both to New York and to Bridgeport before opening in 1856 the firm of Brewster & Co., of Broome Street, New York. Brewster wagons and carriages are considered among the finest ever made in this country. Between 1915 and 1925 the company built motor cars, and finally, in 1926, the firm was purchased by Rolls Royce to build car bodies. This appealing print illustrates neither wagons, sulkies, nor coaches. It shows only the great trotters of the moment and recent past, George M. Patchen, Lady Suffolk, Princess, Ethan Allen, and, of course, Flora Temple—all accurately delineated. The manufacturer obviously trades upon the common assumption of the period—fine horses deserved to pull good wagons.

The most famous sire of trotting horses in the nineteenth century was unquestionably Hambletonian, and in the Peters Collection are two lithographed portraits of him both issued in 1866. The first is after a painting by Theodore Marsden, drawn on stone by Henry A. Thomas, and published by Henry C. Eno, of New York. Hambletonian was a horse who always drew superlatives. One contemporary description noted that his coat was the "brightest of bays" and glistened "like the sheen of satin." His legs were without blemish

6. Troye's painting of Flora Temple, according to Busbey, "Trotting Horse," *Harper's New Monthly*, vol. 47, p. 608, represented her "standing in the open pasture, her first-born, a graceful colt, by her side." Although apparently bred many times, Flora produced only twice.

GEO. M. PATCHEN.   LADY SUFFOLK.   PRINCESS.   ETHAN ALLEN.   FLORA TEMPLE.

TROTTING GALLERY

FROM A PICTURE BY W. F. ATTWOOD. 1860.

PUBLISHED BY BREWSTER & CO., CARRIAGE MAKERS.

Nos 372 & 374 BROOME, COR. OF MOTT STREETS, NEW YORK.

First Class Road and Trotting Wagons a Speciality.

GEO. M. PATCHEN.

LADY SUFFOLK.

ETHAN ALLEN.

PRINCESS.

FLORA TEMPLE.

and had great muscular power, "shining like bars of polished steel."[7] Frank Forester endorsed this account as the finest ever written in describing Hambletonian, and Eno's print after Marsden's painting illustrates well the satiny, shining, muscular qualities of the horse. Hambletonian was foaled in 1849 and became, not a noted track performer, but rather the greatest begetter of the Messenger strain ever to stand stud during the nineteenth century. The prolific stallion carried the blood of Imported Messenger plus that of Bellfounder through the Charles Kent mare, and he is surely unsurpassed as a progenitor of harness horses. In 1897 it was accepted as fact that "the great mass of trotters of today have more or less of his blood in their veins, and in a very short time that blood will abound in greater or less strength in every American trotter."[8] By the time he was a three-year-old this prodigious and profitable stallion had "covered seventeen mares, thirteen of whom produced foals. From that time forward he became entirely devoted to the harem, and is now regarded as the progenitor of the best trotting horses in the world." In his lifetime Hambletonian "covered over seventeen-hundred mares and is known to have been the sire of twelve hundred and forty, netting his owner nearly $200,000."[9] His get were celebrated horses of the quality of Dexter, George Wilkes, Bruno, Brunette, Major Winfield, Volunteer, and Alexander's Abdallah. William Rysdyk had paid $125 for Hambletonian, and before the horse died in 1876 he was receiving $500 a stand as a stud fee. Printmakers and horsemen alike saw in Hambletonian that "he was all action."[10]

Another print, entitled "Rysdyk's Hambletonian," was published in 1866 by John J. Olone. Lithographed in color by Henry C. Eno after a painting by James Wright, this portrait suggests the epitome of stabling facilities, and properly so, for housed within was the finest stallion yet produced by American breeders. The influence of a print of this type as a

---

7. As quoted by *Frank Forester*, vol. 2, p. 259, from a description which appeared in *The Turf, Field and Farm*, February 12, 1869.   8. Wallace, *Horse of America*, p. 273.   9. *Frank Forester*, vol. 2, p. 260.   10. Wallace, *Horse of America*, p. 269.

HAMBLETONIAN.
THE PROPERTY OF W^M M. RYSDYK OF CHESTER, ORANGE COUNTY, NEW YORK.

Was sired by old Abdallah, he by Mambrino, and he by imported Messenger. His dam was the Charles Kent mare by imported Bellfounder; grand dam, old One Eye by old Hambletonian, and he by imported Messenger; and his dam also by imported Messenger, and the dam of old One Eye was by imported Messenger.

CHS S. HUMPHREY'S PINXT.   Entered according to act of Congress, in the year 1866, by Henry C. Eno, in the Clerk's Office of the District Court of the United States, for the Southern District of New York.   LITH. & PRINTED IN COLORS BY H.C. ENO, 37 PARK ROW, N.Y.

VOLUNTEER.

Sired by Rysdyk's Hambletonian, Dam by Young Patriot &c.&c.

PROPERTY OF ALDEN GOLDSMITH, BLOOMING GROVE ORANGE C? N.Y.

yardstick of improved horse care is hard to assess. In general it might be assumed that horse owners, seeing Hambletonian's accommodations, would model their horse stalls accordingly. The print, as an example of good practice, contains most of the appurtenances considered necessary for proper horse maintenance. These included a good window for ventilation, well-designed mangers, and hard-finished, whitewashed walls. "Exceedingly objectionable," however, according to Frank Forester, was the planked flooring commonly used in America. Invariably such a floor held moisture, became saturated with ammonia, "offend the air," and—worst—tended "to produce heat in the feet of the animal." Properly, stall litter is noticeably lacking, and the dictum of cleanliness and order as a prerequisite of equine management is an idea clearly conveyed.[11]

James Wright, on whose painting the lithograph is based, was a frequent exhibitor at the American Art Union and the National Academy. His work includes landscapes, still lifes, marine views, and portraiture. His version of Hambletonian captured especially well the solid power of the animal. Interestingly, William Rysdyk's countenance and character remained, from rendering to rendering of Hambletonian, strikingly consistent.[12]

Volunteer, Hambletonian's famous son, is the subject of another Eno print in the Peters Collection. This portrait is after a painting by Charles S. Humphreys and was put on stone by Henry Thomas in 1864. Although not a particularly handsome rendering of the horse, it does, however, emphasize the strength and power of the Hambletonian line. At the time of the appearance of this print, Volunteer's fame was only just established, and it was not until the early 1870s that he began to rival his sire as a producer of fine stock. When Hambletonian died in 1876, horsemen proclaimed Volunteer "the greatest living sire of trotters."[13] The prints by Eno of Hambletonian and Volunteer are also colorful reminders that Orange County, New York, was a center of fine stud farms and good trotting stock. Little

11. *Frank Forester*, vol. 2, pp. 416–417.   12. Groce and Wallace, *New-York Historical Society's Dictionary of Artists*, p. 705.   13. Wallace, *Horse of America*, p. 303.

is known of the recorders of this portrait of Volunteer. Humphreys, as pointed out previously, painted portraits human and otherwise, while, according to the census of 1860, Henry Thomas was employed as an engraver living in the city of New York. Of the two prints of Volunteer in the Peters Collection the more appealing is the view already discussed (pp. 118–119) of horse, wagon, and owner at a fast trot, also after a painting by Humphreys. In his standing portrait Humphreys presents simply a well-muscled view of a sturdy stud. When considered together, however, the two prints give a full interpretation of the horse—strong, well formed, elegant, and fast.[14]

The Mambrinos had been the pioneer trotting stock in Kentucky, and Mambrino Chief was the founder of the breed and the leading head of the tribe. In 1867 J. Cameron produced a colored lithograph of Mambrino Champion. This print is based on Cameron's painting and is a proof before letter. (Currier & Ives had in 1867 published a large portrait by Cameron entitled "Trotting Stallion Mambrino Champion.") Cameron, hunchbacked and an inveterate drinker, was one of the century's best horse portraitists, and, although he worked mostly for Currier & Ives, he at times worked on his own. Mambrino Champion, so appealing in Cameron's print, was foaled in 1861. His time of 39 seconds over the last quarter mile at the Goshen Horse Fair in 1866 was considered a notable achievement.[15]

Other important Kentucky and Tennessee horses were frequently the subject of lithographs. An untitled and undated black-and-white lithograph, drawn from life by A. C. Webb, of Nashville, shows a pleasing pasture with three black horses dominating the landscape. The horses are the progeny of Dictator and George Wilkes, each of whom were sons of Hambletonian. Dictator was taken to Kentucky briefly in 1876 and permanently in 1883. George Wilkes first stood stud in Lexington in 1873, and after that date became a prolific sire of standardbred performers.[16]

14. Groce and Wallace, *New-York Historical Society's Dictionary of Artists*, p. 624.   15. Wallace, *Horse of America*, pp. 315–320.   16. See "Among the Blue-Grass Trotters," *Harper's New Monthly Magazine*, vol. 67, pp. 715–730.

Untitled [Mambrino Champion].

Untitled. A. C. Webb, Nashville.

ENGRAVED & PRINTED BY HOMER LEE & CO. NEW YORK.

COPYRIGHTED 1878 BY VACUUM OIL CO. ROCHESTER N.Y.

BEST TIME
ON RECORD 2.13¼ BUFFALO, N.Y.
AUG 3RD 1878

RARUS.

PUBLISHED BY
VACUUM OIL COMPANY
ROCHESTER N.

The Vacuum Oil Company's advertising folios portrayed the giants of the trotting turf; their spirited view of Jay Eye See has already been discussed in a previous chapter. Their portrait of Rarus recalls the date of his record mile, August 3, 1878, and the caption "Best Time on Record" was superfluous information to informed followers of the track. The exciting view by Haskell of Rarus among the trotters in harness again provides a comparison for a full interpretation of the horse. This bay gelding was one of the many outstanding trotters purchased by Robert Bonner. The splendid time made by Rarus, however, stood for only a year before it was eclipsed. On this occasion General Grant, just home from a world cruise, was in the stands on October 25, 1879, at Oakland, California, when St. Julien trotted the mile in 2:12¾. The San Francisco Bulletin Company, as a result of the race, published a lithograph by E. Bosqui & Co. in 1880. St. Julien was now the fastest trotter in the world, and his success was additional proof of the sound characteristics of the Messenger-Hambletonian strain. St. Julien's sire had been Volunteer, the prolific son of Hambletonian.[17] The portrait in the Peters Collection tends to strip away the romantic and dashing image of the horse as portrayed in Scott Leighton's painting of this champion. Leighton's oil, now in the collections of the Hall of Fame of the Trotter at Goshen, New York, shows St. Julien fully extended and driven by Orrin Hickok, Wild Bill's brother.

The great age of lithography was coming to a close in 1885 when Mayer, Merkle & Ottman published their black-and-white print of Wedgewood 692. This horse was one of the most accomplished sons of the outstanding sire, Belmont. Wedgewood was advertised as a stud in 1886, and his prowess was based on his record as a trotter and on his feat of winning "every race in the Grand Circuit of 1880, a performance never equalled by any other stallion." Foaled in 1871, he is credited with having produced 31 standard performers

17. See the *Commercial Advertiser* (Buffalo), August 5, 1878, and the *American Agriculturist*, vol. 42 (August 1883), p. 355, for Rarus' record trot; see also, Hugh Craig, "American Horses," *Harper's New Monthly*, vol. 67, p. 346.

ST. JULIEN. 2:12½. OAKLAND, CAL. Oct. 25. 1879.

St. Julien. San Francisco Bulletin Company, 1880.

WEDGEWOOD'S ROLL OF HONOR.

Of the First Ten Foals came the following:

CONWAY,	2.8½	NUGGET,	2.26½
ULVA,	2.27½	CONNAUGHT,	2.24
FAVONIA,	2.27½	JESUIT,	2.32½
MERSBURG,	2.40	MAYENNE,	

Wedgewood sired but seventeen foals in Kentucky, of which three are dead, five are in the 2.30 list, and the balance are in the stud of prominent breeders and were never developed.

WEDGEWOOD 692.

BY BELMONT — WOODBINE,

RECORD 2.19.

PROPERTY OF

HERMITAGE STUD,

NASHVILLE, TENN.

(horses that had made or bettered 2:30 for the mile), and over the course of two generations his progeny sired a total of 91. This handsome example of lithographic advertising on
behalf of the Hermitage Stud, of Nashville, Tennessee, depicts Wedgewood 692 precisely
as we would expect—strong, powerful, and lordly, a virile brute who was the king of all
he surveyed.[18]

The final standing portrait in the Peters Collection is a colored lithograph of Cresceus
published by the Frontier Lithography Co. in 1903, which appeared in the same year on
the cover of *Horse World*. In 1902 Cresceus was the subject of a biography by John Mc-
Cartney entitled *The Story of a Great Horse*. This account traces him from a foal in 1894
on the Ketchum farm near Toledo through his rapid early training and performances. The
first high point of his career was in 1901, when he trotted a record-shattering 2:02¼ on the
mile track at Columbus, Ohio. His subsequent record-breaking 1:59¾ took place in 1903
—and all this was accomplished in his first seven years! His progress on the track was in
startling contrast to Hiram Woodruff's doctrines of the early nineteenth century that
stressed the slow training and development of the trotter. In seven years Cresceus went to
the post 61 times: he finished first 42 times, second 14 times, third 4 times, and fourth 1
time. In this brief period he won over $102,851, averaging per year more money earned
than any stallion had ever won in any single year of competition. The importance of this
portrait of Cresceus is its photographic character. The idealized qualities of the champion
trotter, so much a part of early lithographic horse portraiture, are stripped away. The portrait of Cresceus is the latest in date of the trotting prints in the Peters Collection, and it is
a fitting climax to a gallery of splendid trotters because it commemorates the great goal
finally achieved—the posting of a sub-two-minute mile.[19]

18. From an advertisement entitled "The Great Campaigner Wedgewood, 692" recurring throughout *Wallace's Monthly* (1886) that gave the stallion's terms $100 "due at time of service."   19. John McCartney, *The Story of a Great Horse, Cresceus, 2:02¼* (Indianapolis, 1902).

· CRESCEUS ·
1.59 ¾

THE COVER OF THIS NUMBER OF THE HORSE WORLD
AND ALL OF THE INSERTS WERE LITHOGRAPHED BY THE
FRONTIER LITHOGRAPH CO.
BUFFALO, N.Y.

60.3621

FRONTIER LITHOGRAPH CO.
BUFFALO, N.Y.
HIGH GRADE LITHOGRAPHIC WORK OF ALL KIN
WRITE FOR SAMPLES AND PRICES.

Overall, the portraits of trotters tend to be stiff and less appealing than the livelier views of trotters in action. The standing portrait is merely an extension of the English tradition of horse paintings and horse prints, and, in the lithographic interpretation of the trotter, Americans in the nineteenth century did not improve on their older model. Somehow the thoroughbred runner or hunter seemed perfectly acceptable in portrait pose, a quality not transmitted by the trotter, whose singular beauty shines most clearly only when translated in terms of his gait and motion.

St. PATRICK.

This celebrated imported Horse

will stand for the season at the stable of the subscriber in the town of Rotterdam, every day in the week except Fridays and Saturdays, on which days he will stand at Neilson Frier's, in same town; and will be let to mares on the following terms:--- Single leap, $4. Season, $7. Insurance, $12.--- Season to end on the 7th day of July next.

St. PATRICK

was got by the famous Race horse Richmond; his

dam by *Challenger*, who was got by *Tom Tug*, out of *Mary Gray*; *Tom Tug* was by *King Herod*, out of *Legacy*; *Mary Gray* by *Friar*: dam *Timante*, by *Tim*, out of sister to *Noble*, by *Gamahoe*. *Richmond* was got by *Young Wood Pecker*, out of *Platina*, sister to *Silver*.

St. PATRICK was bred by the Marquis of

Donegal, and imported from Ireland to America when two years old; is a Chesnut Sorrel, 15 hands high, and of very superior action.

His performances were of the first order while on the Turf; at Cornwell, Upper Canada, he ran a second two mile heat, carrying 143 lbs., in 3 minutes and 52 seconds.

C. CHISM.

Rotterdam, May 12th, 1838.

The last distinct category among the Peters prints illustrating the trotting horse is a miscellany of handbills and broadsides. From the seventeenth century to the close of the nineteenth the methods and the media for advertising horses either for sale or for stud changed very little. Books dealing with the breeding and development of trotting horses as late as 1906 still advised their readers always, as had long been the practice, to patronize local newspapers, including nearby horse papers. It was always wise to advertise in at least one or more journals of national reputation devoted to turf news. "This," according to the best experience, "keeps your horse before the general public, and will not only secure you enough extra mares to pay for your advertising but will augment the reputation of your stallion and increase the selling price of his colts, when they come on."[1]

The earliest of the handbills in the Peters Collection boldly advertises an auction of blooded stock for sale under the direction of the "New-York Tattersalls." The handbill was engraved and signed by E. Forbes, wood engraver, and was printed by Jared W. Bell in New York on June 1, 1837.

Cultural independence from England was a constant theme in the early United States, but in the development of fine horseflesh American breeders subordinated their prejudices. They had long imported good English stallions, but now they also traded upon the name of Tattersalls, the most respected horse-auction house in England. In the horse world to evoke the name of Richard Tattersall and his sons was synonymous with integrity and quality, for the Tattersalls had a reputation that had been in the making since the mid-eighteenth-century. At Snedicor's in June of 1837, as the handbill announces, blooded horses by Duroc were available, as well as the progeny of unions that looked directly to Imported Messenger and American Eclipse. The stallions Talma and Bravo, bred of New York and Virginia stock, were being offered, and, in addition, there were in various stages of training a number of two- to six-year-olds—mostly runners—to be auctioned.

1. John Bradburn, *Breeding and Developing the Trotter* (Boston, 1906), p. 75.

Less sophisticated is an advertisement printed at Rotterdam, New York. A wood engraving, signed simply "Anderson" and dated May 12, 1838, announces the availability of St. Patrick as a stud. Purportedly, St. Patrick was an imported English stallion. He was presumed, and billed, as the son of the splendid English racehorse, Richmond. He had been bred, so the broadside attests, by the Marquis of Donegal. Frank Forester, however, makes no mention of St. Patrick among imported stallions, nor does *Wallace's American Stud-Book* mention him.[2] In evaluating St. Patrick, the modest amount of his stud fee must be weighed against the appeal of having your mare bred to a "genuine" Irish stallion. That St. Patrick was a fraud does not necessarily follow, although breeders were wise if they recalled Frank Forester's admonition that the title of many thoroughbreds had been "made to pass muster . . . on the bare assertion of their importers." Performance was, after all, the surest test of American pedigreed stock.[3] (It is notable that none of St. Patrick's progeny are listed in the Rotterdam broadside!)

Another woodblock engraving printed in Rotterdam, New York, is a simple rural announcement proclaiming in bold type **"Vendue."** It is dated November 13, 1838, and advertises "HORSES" and, less prominently, harness, wagons, and sheep. By contrast to the stud announcement, this ephemeral survival documents a Saturday morning sale to be held by D. D. Campbell on November 24, 1838, at Rotterdam in upstate New York; there are no vignettes, and one can only surmise that the horses offered may have been "good roadsters" to compliment the "Pleasure Waggons" also being sold that day. Little imagination is needed to visualize Campbell's sale taking place in any one of the crisp, neat towns of western and upstate New York, characterized by quiet "villas, and gardens, and rows of

2. John H. Wallace, *Wallace's American Stud-Book* (New York, 1867).   3. Henry William Herbert [Frank Forester], *Frank Forester's Horse and Horsemanship of the United States and the British Provinces of North America* (New York, 1871), vol. 1, p. 500; John H. Wallace, *The Horse of America* (New York, 1897), p. 512.

trees, and green paddocks for sleek horses and cows, and stylish equipages driving about making calls."[4]

In 1849 a broadside printed by Jared W. Bell announced that the famous and well-known horse, Trustee, would stand for mares at the stable of Henry Booth in Morrisania. The fee was $30, and the exact location of Booth's stable was about a mile from Harlem Bridge. Years before at Morven, his family seat near Princeton, New Jersey, the distinguished naval officer, Robert Stockton, had for a time imported, bred, and raced blooded English horses. In 1835, temporarily retired from his naval career, Stockton had brought Trustee to the United States, and by 1849 this English stallion was billed "throughout the Union as one of the finest Horses ever imported." He was noted particularly for his "size, symmetry, action and blood." He was, as the broadside indicated, the ingredient that American horsemen felt necessary "to improve the breed of horses not only for the turf but for the road and general use."

In Victorian America horse breeders almost to a man (Hiram Woodruff was an exception) believed that the best way to produce trotters was to infuse as much running blood as possible at every cross. Clearly, when establishing a good line of trotters the thoroughbred (in American parlance an English running horse) was the essential element, the one factor that should appear in every pedigree. By the end of the century, however, the vogue of matching the running stallion to the sound trotting mare had been largely replaced by the success of systematically breeding proven performers, and, to eliminate throwbacks, this through at least five generations. Trustee had been one of many English imports whose stud performances had given support to the idée fixe that running blood alone produced fine trotters. For example, had not the foal resulting from Trustee's union with the trotting mare Fanny Pullen, the gelding Trustee, become the first horse to trot 20 miles in an hour?

4. William Chambers, *Things as They Are in America* (London, 1854), p. 165.

Overlooked by most enthusiasts, however, was the fact that the gelding Trustee was the only trotter of consequence sired by his imported namesake and, furthermore, that no horse carrying Trustee blood had yet distinguished itself as a sire or a dam of performers for the trotting track. By the end of the nineteenth century the concept that thoroughbred blood was the foundation for a good trotter had been replaced by the careful administration of the axiom that like begets like. In a negative way Trustee's stud career helped to validate this rule.[5]

The final broadside in the Peters Collection is a colorful race poster printed by Currier & Ives on the order of a theatrical playbill, which includes a small vignette entitled "A Good Race, Well Won." The poster was a blank, and the vignette a standard scene; the purchaser simply filled in the meet dates. Moreover, the vignette had no relationship either to the real appearance of Charter Oak Park or to the Hartford Races in the late August of 1889, which the broadside advertised. In 1889 the *Hartford Courant* carried detailed accounts of the races that this handbill drummed. These descriptions stressed the presence of photographers and the use of telephonic communication between the judges' stand and the press tent. By 1889 most trackgoers realized the unreality of the print as a true picture of what had become a very commercialized sport. Despite this, for nearly sixty years Americans, whether at the track or on the road, in summer or in winter, had had the fetlock fever, a disease of long duration which the printmakers had helped prolong with countless views of the trotting horse on the road, under saddle, in harness, hitched to wagon, in portraiture, and in a variety of broadsides. These lithographs as a group, in spite of their inaccuracy and unreality, attest a very important aspect of the American character. Tocqueville, early in the nineteenth century, had stated that Americans "want something productive and ·substantial in their pleasures; they want to mix actual fruition with their joy." In this general statement he had hit upon the fascination that the trotting horse held

5. Wallace, *Horse of America*, p. 512. For Trustee's obituary, see *The New York Daily Times*, September 3, 1856.

for the average American. The trotter was the embodiment of Tocqueville's analysis—productive, always fun, and, without question, one of the most useful animals ever perfected by any age.[6]

6. *The Hartford Courant*, August 28–31, 1889; Alexis de Tocqueville, *Democracy in America*, edit. Phillip Bradley (New York, 1945), vol. 2, p. 211.

BLOODED STOCK.

FOR SALE BY AUCTION,

UNDER THE DIRECTION OF THE PROPRIETORS OF THE "NEW-YORK TATTERSALLS,"

AT MR. JOHN R. SNEDICOR'S,

NEAR THE UNION COURSE, LONG ISLAND,

On FRIDAY, June 2, 1837, at 10 o'clock, A. M.

THE FOLLOWING BLOOD HORSES:

No. 1. SPORTSMISTRESS, gr. m., bred by General Coles, of Dosoris, L. I., foaled 1818, got by *Old Hickory*, by *Imported Whip*, her dam *Miller's Damsel*, (by *Imported Messenger*,) the dam of *American Eclipse, &c.*

No. 2. GULNARE, gr. m., bred by General Coles, foaled 1824, by *Duroc*, sire of *American Eclipse*, dam *Sportsmistress*.

No. 3. THE JEWESS, gr. m. foaled 1831, by *Henry*, dam *Gulnare*.

STALLIONS.

No. 4. TALMA, gr. h. 16 hands high, foaled 1833, by *Henry*, dam *Sportmistress*, which makes him full brother to *Alice Grey*, who beat, with all ease, *Black Maria*, over the Union Course, in 7:56—7:50. She was the best get of *Henry*.

No. 5. BRAVO, b. h., 16 hands high, foaled 1829, by *Henry*, dam *Gulnare*, by *Duroc*.

IN TRAINING.

No. 6. G. c., 16 hands high, foaled 1833, got by *Henry*, out of *Sportsmistress*. He is a full brother to *Alice Grey*, and promises to make a race horse.

No. 7. Ch. c., 15½ hands high, foaled 1833, bred by John N. Lloyd, Esq., of Lloyd's Neck, L. I., (the breeder of *Post Boy, Tarquin,* and *Robin Hood*,) was got by *Talma*, out of *Dove*, by *Duroc*. She is full sister to *Cock of the Rock*, and *Young Romp*; he is very promising.

No. 8. G. c., foaled 1834, got by the race horse *Flying Childers*, he by *Sir Archie*, out of *Gulnare, by Duroc*. This colt is engaged in a stake over the Union Course, First Spring Meeting, 18 subs., and First Fall Meeting, 11 subs.

No. 9. Ch. c., foaled 1836, by *Gohanna*, out of *Gulnare*. He is engaged in a stake to be run over the Kendall Course,

No. 10&11. Spring of 1839. $1,000 entrance, $250 forfeit.

Hall's Stock, SURPRISE and BAY FILLY.

No. 12. A SORREL MARE, 6 years old, bred by Mr. Abraham Laurence, out of a full-blooded Mare, got by *Old Duroc*, her dam by *Old Messenger*. Further particulars at sale.

No. 13. A BAY HORSE, 3 years old, got by *Andrew*, dam *Miss Fisher*, (bred by H. N. Cruger, Esq.) *Miss Fisher*, by *John Richards*, dam by Gen. Coles' *Hamiltonian*, G. D. *Imp*, by *Cottager*, G. G. D. by *Tentham*, G. G. G. D. by *Henricus*, G. G. G. G. D. by *Regulus, &c.*

JOHN W. WATSON & CO., 446 Broadway.

June 1, 1837.

PRINTED BY J. W. BELL, 17 ANN-STREET, NEW-YORK.

THE HORSE.

TRUSTEE,

The Sire of Fashion, Revenue, &c. &c.

ALSO, IS THE SIRE OF THE CELEBRATED

TROTTING HORSE TRUSTEE

Who trotted *TWENTY MILES WITHIN THE HOUR*, last fall, over the Union Course, heavy sums being staked against his performance of that distance within the hour. The dam of trotting Trustee is the only trotting mare Trustee ever served.

This magnificent Race Horse and Stallion will stand for Mares, the present Season, at the Stable of **HENRY BOOTH, FLAT-FIELD, Morrisania,**

ONE MILE FROM HARLEM BRIDGE, AT THIRTY DOLLARS.

Is known throughout the Union as one of the finest Horses ever imported from England. His size, symmetry, action, and blood, admirably qualify him to improve the breed of Horses, not only for the Turf, but for the Road and general use. The FIRST PREMIUM was awarded to TRUSTEE, as the best bred Stallion, by the American Institute at their Agricultural Fair in 1847; and also a Premium was awarded him at the Agricultural Fair of Westchester County the same year.

TRUSTEE's terms will be Thirty Dollars the SEASON,

Which will commence on the 1st of March and terminate on the 1st July, 1849. The Money to be paid before the Mares are taken away. GOOD PASTURE provided for Mares and every attention paid to their safety, but no liability for accidents and escapes.

HENRY BOOTH.

Flat-Field, Morrisiana Village, February, 1849.

TRUSTEE

PEDIGREE AND PERFORMANCES OF TRUSTEE.

TRUSTEE, a ch. h., foaled in 1829, and bred by W. Ridsdale, was got by Catton, out of Emma, by Whisker, (brother to Whalebone, Woful, Wire, &c., and the sire of Memnon, the Colonel,) Gilsdale Fairy, by Hermes, out of Vicissitude, by Pipator—Beatrice by Sir Peter, &c., &c. (See Stud Book.)

Catton, sire of Trustee, was got by Golumpus, own brother to Hedley and Wanderer—his dam, Lucy Gray, by Timothy, (by Delphini, out of Cora by Matchem,) grandam Lucy, by Florizel, out of Phrenzy by Eclipse. During his career he won 14 successive races, and walked over one. As will be seen by the Calendar, he was one of the best four milers of his day, and is the sire of many well known winners, among whom are Tarrare, winner of the St. Leger, Anna, sister to Tarrare, David, Contest, Minster, Diana, Lady Charlotte, Mundig, &c. &c. (See Wetherby's Racing Calendar.)

At the Epson Meeting, 1835, Mundig, own brother to Trustee, won the Derby Stakes, 3 years old, carrying 8 st. 7 lb. mile and a half—128 subscribers, 50 to 1 against Mundig. At the Newmarket Craven Meeting, Ibrahim, Selinus, Cariolanus by Emilus, &c. 7 to 4 against Ibrahim, 3 to 1 against Ascot, 6 to 1 against Mundig. Ascot came in second, Ibrahim not placed.

At Epsom Meeting, in the spring of 1832, Trustee ran third to St. Giles, (St. Giles, Margrave, and Trustee, at this time all belonged to the same owners, Gully & Ridsdale,) for the Derby Stakes, 101 subscribers, beating Margrave, (winner of the St. Leger stakes, both at Doncaster and Newmarket,) Beiram, (winner of the July and Pendergast stakes,) Kate, Emiliana, Von Compos, Rounceval, Mixbury, and 13 others—23 having started. After this race Trustee was purchased by the Duke of Cleaveland for 2,000 guineas.

At Doncaster, the same year, he was beaten by Margrave and Birdcatcher, none others placed; 75 subscribers.

At the Newmarket Houghton Meeting, same year, Trustee, at 8 st. 4 lb., ridden by Chiffney, beat Mr. Grevil's Dryad, 7 st. 10 lb., D. M., in a match, 300 sovereigns a side, h. ft.

At the Newmarket Craven Meeting, 1833, Trustee ran second to Rounceval, (whom he had previously beaten) for the Oatland stakes, D. I. 15 subscribers; beating Consol, Beiram, Bazarre, Lady Fly, Agent, and Hokee Pokee.

At the same Meeting he won the Claret stakes of 200 sovereigns, each h. ft., carrying 8 st. 7 lb., D. I., beating Minster, Beiram, and Margrave, second time; even betting on Trustee.

At Newmarket first Spring Meeting, he beat Lord Conyngham's Minster, 8 st. 7 each, in a Match across the flat, 20 sovereigns h. ft. 7 to 4 on Trustee.

At York August Meeting same year, he was beaten by Voluna, for the great subscription : 2 miles, 11 subscribers ; 5 to 2 on Trustee.

At the same meeting Trustee was beaten by Voltri and Tilbo, carrying 8 st. 3 lb. : 2 miles.

At the Doncaster September meeting he won the Claret stakes, carrying 8 st. 4 lb. : 2 miles, 3 subs., beating Pickpocket by St. Patrick, &c.

At the Newmarket Craven meeting, 1834, Trustee ran second to Sir Mark Wood's Oaks Filly Vespa, D. I., carrying 8 st. 10 lb., and beating Lottery out of Pledge, Lord Exeter's Galata, (winner of the Oaks,) Chantilly, Arm by Catton, and Col. Peel's Malibran ; 9 to 2 against Trustee.

At the Newmarket first Spring Meeting, 1835, having stood his training, he was run against and beaten by Col. Peel's Nonsense, and Lord Exeter's Daturn, when Lord Cleaveland ordered him to be sold. Catton, Trustee's sire, had seven winners in the year 1836 on the English Turf, who won twelve prizes. He had 32 of his get entered for the big thing in 1837. In 1835, Catton had six winners, Mundig, Gratus, Contest, Chancellor, Zora, &c., &c., who won ten prizes, including the Derby stakes at Epsom of 3,600*l*, and 600*l*, at Doncaster.

Whisker, the sire of Trustee's dam, Emma, had several fine runners on the English Turf. In 1835, Whisker's get won eleven prizes, including the Gold Cups at Liverpool and Northallerton.

The number in brackets at the end of each catalog entry refers to the page in this book on which the print is reproduced. Prints without bracketed page numbers are not illustrated.

The Trotter and the Road

1. Andrew Jackson Jr. / Owned by Arthur H. Mann, / Baltimore.
Black-and-white lithograph by A. Hoen & Co., Baltimore, from a painting by E. Clarkson, Philadelphia. Undated. 19¼ x 24⅝ in. Cat. no. 60.3569. SI photo 56172. [5]

2. Road Scenes, No. 1. / "The Shed"
Colored lithograph by Endicott & Co., New York, from a painting by J. A. Oertel; signed in lower-left corner "J. A. Oertel Dec. 1861." Published by Brewster & Co., of Broome St., New York. 1862. 19¾ x 31¾ in. Cat. no. 60.3563. SI photo 56177. [facing p. 1]

3. "Taking the Reins" / Drawn by John W. Ehninger. / The celebrated trotting-horse Dexter driven by General Grant / and Robert Bonner Esq. owner of Dexter and proprietor of the N.Y. Ledger.
Photomechanical reproduction, from a photograph by W. Kurtz, New York; signed in lower left corner "John W. Ehninger." 1869. 15¾ x 20⅞ in. Cat. no. 60.3587. SI photo 56201. [19]

4. Watering Place on the Road.
Colored lithograph. Published by Thomas Kelly, New York. 1870. 17⅞ x 24½ in. Cat. no. 60.3553. SI photo 56181. [6]

5. Trotting Cracks of Philadelphia Returning from the Race at Point Breeze Park, / Having a Brush Past Turner's Hotel, Rope Ferry Road, Philadelphia, 1870. / Respectfully Dedicated to the Lovers of Horses and the Sporting Public in general by the Publisher.

Colored lithograph. Published by H. Pharazyn, Philadelphia. 1870. 21⅛ x 29 in. Cat. no. 60.3557. SI photo 56239. [20]

6. Going to the Trot.
Colored lithograph printed and published by Thomas Kelly, New York. 1870. 18⅛ x 24⅞ in. Cat. no. 60.3556. SI photo 56174. [13]

7. Trotting Cracks on the Road / Scene—Harlem Lane.
Colored lithograph published by Thomas Kelly, New York. 1870. 18¼ x 24¾ in. Cat. no. 60.3560. SI photo 56236. [15]

8. Fast Horses, of N.Y. Scene Harlem Lane N.Y.
Colored lithograph, from an original sketch by J. Beard. Published by Thomas Kelly, New York. 1871. 17⅞ x 24⅞ in. Cat. no. 60.3559. SI photo 56175. [21]

9. Leaving Brighton Hotel for the Mill-Dam / Summer.
Colored lithograph, signed in lower right corner "E. R. Howe del." Published by Haskell & Allen Boston. 1871. 18¼ x 25¼ in. Cat. no. 60.3552. SI photo 56205. [24]

10. Trotting Cracks on the Brighton Road. / (Scene, Mile Ground.)
Colored lithograph. Published by Haskell & Allen, Boston. 1872. 20¼ x 26 in. Cat. no. 60.3554. SI photo 56240. [22]

11. Winter. / Going to a Christmas Party.
Colored lithograph. Published and printed by J. H. Bufford, Boston. Undated. 10½ x 13¾ in. Cat. no. 60.3577. SI photo 56167. [30]

12. Sleigh Race.
Artist, publisher, place, and date of publication unknown. 11 x 16⅜ in. Cat. no. 60.3585. SI photo 56162.

13. Leaving Brighton Hotel for the Mill-Dam / Winter.
Colored lithograph. Published by Haskell & Allen, Boston.
1871. 21 x 25⅛ in. Cat. no. 60.3558. SI photo 56235.   [25]

14. Fearnaught Stallions, / Owned by David Nevins Jr.,
Framingham, Mass. / From the Original Painti[ng] by
S[cott Leighto]n / Fearnaught Boy by the Old Horse, Lan-
cet by [Ju]nior.
Colored lithograph, signed in lower right corner "L. G.
Eaton. Lith." Published by Haskell & Allen, Boston. 1875.
18 x 25⅛ in. Cat. no. 60.3555. SI photo 56183.   [34]

15. Fearnaught Stallions, / Owned by David Nevins Jr.,
Framingham, Mass. / From the Original Painting by Scott
Leighton / Fearnaught Boy by the Old Horse; Lancet by
Junior.
Colored lithograph. Published by Haskell & Allen, Boston.
1875. 11 x 14 in. Cat. no. 60.3605. SI photo 56247.

16. Untitled.
Colored lithograph, signed in lower left corner "E. R.
Howe." Place and date of publication unknown. 17½ x 25¾
in. Cat. no. 60.3539. SI photo 56291.

17. Untitled.
Colored lithograph. Copyrighted by Haskell & Allen, Boston. 1877. 17½ x 35¾ in. Cat. no. 60.3540. SI photo 56508.

18. Untitled.
Colored lithograph, signed in lower right corner "J. Came-
ron." Place and date of publication unknown. 10¾ x 15 in.
Cat. no. 60.3578. SI photo 56163.   [35]

19. A Home in the Country / Winter.
Colored lithograph. Published by Thomas Kelly, New York.
Undated. 17½ x 24½ in. Cat. no. 60.2639. SI photo 55703.
[27]

20. Winter in the Country.—The Farmers Home.
Colored lithograph. Published by Charles Brothers, New
York; drawn and printed by Charles Hart, New York. Un-
dated. 17 x 24 in. Cat. no. 60.2638. SI photo 60420B.   [28]

21. Winter Scene in the Country.
Colored lithograph. Published by J. Kelly & Sons, Philadelphia and New York; printed by Wm. C. Robertson, New
York. Undated. 17⅛ x 24¾ in. Cat. no. 63.184. SI photo
60985.   [29]

22. Winter.
Colored lithograph. Published by Haskell & Allen, Boston.
Undated. 17¼ x 24³⁄₁₆ in. Cat. no. 63.183.
SI photo 60985A.   [32]

23. Winter Pleasure in the Country.
Colored lithograph, signed in lower right corner "F. Fudes"
(?). Published by Kimmel & Forster, New York. Undated.
10 x 13½ in. Cat. no. 60.2645. SI photo 60421.   [31]

24. A Merry Christmas, / A Happy New-Year.
Colored lithograph, marked in lower right corner. B.
Published by Hughes & Johnson, Chicago. Undated. 13¼ x
12¾ in. Cat. no. 60.2646. SI photo 60424B.   [33]

25. No. 1! and *northin* else.
Black-and-white lithograph. Printed by F. & S. Palmer, New
York. Undated. 11¼ x 15⅝ in. Cat. no. 60.3580. SI photo
56161.

26. Take ca-are what ar-ye 'bout. / No. 2.
Black-and-white lithograph. Printed and published by F. &
S. Palmer, New York. Undated. 10⅝ x 15⅝ in. Cat. no.
60.3581. SI photo 56161.

27. Wake up there! what'r ye' 'bout? / Series No. 3. / No. 3.
Black-and-white lithograph, signed in lower left corner
"O. K." Published by E. Jones & G. W. Newman, New York.
1846. 9¼ x 16¼ in. Cat. no. 60.3582. SI photo 56160.   [38]

28. Two of the B'hoys. / No. 4. Breaking.
Black-and-white lithograph. Printed and published by F. & S. Palmer, New York. Undated. 11 x 16⅛ in. Cat. no. 60.3583. SI photo 56168.   [39]

29. Heigh---gh! Wake up there, what are ye at? / No. 5.
Black-and-white lithograph. Printed and published by F. & S. Palmer, New York. 1846. 10¼ x 15¼ in. Cat. no. 60.3584. SI photo 56169.

30. Deacon Jones' One Hoss Shay. No. 1.
Colored lithograph. Copyrighted by M. J. Warner. 1879. 16⅝ x 24¼ in. Cat. no. 60.3561. SI photo 56176.   [40]

31. Deacon Jones' One Hoss Shay. No. 2.
Colored lithograph. Copyrighted by M. J. Warner. 1879. 18½ x 25½ in. Cat. no. 60.3562. SI photo 562388.   [41]

Trotters under Saddle

32. Columbus / and / Sall[y] Miller. / Columbus, Winner of Tw[e]nty-Two Matches and Purses.
Colored lithograph. Published by / George / Endicott, New York. Undated. 12½ x 20 in. Cat. no. 60.3549. SI photo 56179.   [62]

33. Columbus.
Black-and-white lithograph, after a painting by Richard S. Hillman. Published by Childs & Inman, Philadelphia, Undated. 12½ x 20 in. Cat. no. 60.3602. SI photo 56270.   [63]

34. Lady Suffolk / The Celebrated Trotting Mare. / and her rider, Albert Conklin as they appeared on the BEACON COURSE, HOBOKEN, N. J. on the 12th July, 1843. / From an Original Painting by Robert A. Clarke, by whom this portrait is most respectfully dedicated to / Wm. T. Porter Esq. of N. York.
Colored lithograph, from a painting by Robert A. Clarke.

Published by Lewis & Brown, New York. 1844. 12⅞ x 19 in. Cat. no. 60.3548. SI photo 56171.   [65]

35. Untitled [Lady Suffolk].
Colored lithograph. Artist, publisher, place and date of publication unknown. 12¾ x 19⅛ in. Cat. no. 60.3572. SI photo 56211.

36. Lady Suffolk / The Celebrated Trotting Mare. Foaled in 1833. Died 7 March 1855, / and her rider Albert Concklin as they appeared on the BEACON COURSE, HOBOKEN, N. J. on the 12 July 1843; / from an original painting by Robt. A. Clarke. . . , respectfully dedicated to / Wm. T. Porter Esq. of N. York.
Colored lithograph by George W. Lewis, New York, after a painting by Robert A. Clarke. 1857. 12¼ x 19¼ in. Cat. no. 60.3550. SI photo 56204.   [66]

37. Untitled [Lady Suffolk].
Black-and-white lithograph. Artist, publisher, place and date of publication unknown. 13½ x 17¾ in. Cat. no. 60.3573. SI photo 56212.   [69]

38. Lady Suffolk, / The Renowned Gray Mare, Record 2:26 Ridden by David Bryant. / Copyrighted 1889 — Kinney Bros — High Class Cigarettes.
Colored lithograph. Artist, publisher, and place of publication unknown. 1889. 8 x 10½ in. Cat. no. 60.3637. SI photo 56243.   [70]

39. Celebrated American Trotting Horses.
Black-and-white lithograph by W. H. Rease, Philadelphia, after a painting by Robert A. Clarke. Printed by Wagner & McGuigan, Philadelphia. 1854. 21½ x 38½ in. Cat. no. 60.3532. SI photo 56184.   [71]

40. "Dexter." / Ridden by Mr. BUDD DOBLE. / Foaled April, 1858. Record 2:17¼. Died April, 1888.
Colored, combination lithograph and photograph. Artist,

publisher, date and place of publication unknown. 14½ x 20½ in. Cat. no. 60.3593. SI photo 56230.   [74]

Trotters in Harness

41. Whalebone. / A Noted Horse for Speed & Bottom, Bright Bay, 15 hands 3½ inches high, has strong points & shews great blood. . . .
Black-and-white lithograph by Kennedy & Lucas, Philadelphia, drawn from life and on stone by Richard S. Hillman. Undated. 15¼ x 23 in. Cat. no. 60.3564. SI photo 56165. [76]

42. Untitled.
Black-and-white lithograph by Tappan & Bradford, Boston, after a painting by G. G. Hartwell. Undated. 10 x 17 in. Cat. no. 60.3617. SI photo 56274.

43. Sherman Black Hawk. / Appeared, at the U. S. Agricultural Fair, Held at West Phila. Octr. 8th 1856 and Took the First Premium, of $200.00 Competing with Horses from All Parts of the United States. / Sherman Black Hawk folded [sic] May 30, 1845, the property of B. J. Myrick, Bridport, Vt. / PEDIGREE. Sire, VERMONT BLACK HAWK, Dam by YOUNG HAMILTONIAN [sic], he by Bishop's HAMILTONIAN, by imported MESSINGER [sic], Grand Dam, by imported MATCHUM [sic]. SHERMAN BLACK HAWK is now owned by D. A. BENNITT, Bridport, Vt., and DURA WARREN, Worcester, Mass.
Black-and-white lithograph from a painting by Charles S. Humphreys, by J. H. Bufford, Boston. Undated. 21 x 29½ in. Cat. no. 60.3529. SI photo 56196.   [79]

44. Point Breeze Park.
Colored lithograph after a drawing from nature by James Queen. Published by Thomas Sinclair, Philadelphia. Undated. 7½ x 10⅝ in. Cat. no. 60.3649. SI photo 56782. [80]

45. The Famous Roan Horse Capt. McGowan as he Appeared in his 20th Mile. / In his Great Match Against Time of Trotting in Harness 20 Miles in One Hour Which he Accomplished in 58 Minutes and 25 Seconds / Being the Fastest Time on Record. over the River Side Park, Brighton, Mass. Oct. 31st 1865.
Colored lithograph by J. H. Bufford and Sons, Boston. Published by Samuel Emerson, Riverside Riding Park, Brighton. 1865. 17⅜ x 16⅛ in. Cat. no. 60.3595. SI photo 56513. [83]

46. Dexter, Ethan Allen and Mate / As They Appeared at Fashion Course L.I., June 21st 1867 for a Purse of $2000. / Time 2.15, 2.16, 2.19.
Colored lithograph. Published by Haskell & Allen, Boston. 1872. 17⅞ x 25 in. Cat. no. 60.3530. SI photo 56216.   [86]

47. Dexter, Ethan Allen and Mate / As they appeared at Morristown, N. J. July 4th 1867 for a Purse of $3,500. / Time: 2.20½, 2.20¼, 2.20.
Colored lithograph. Published by Thomas Kelly and printed by Wm. C. Robertson, both of New York. 1868. 17¾ x 24¾ in. Cat. no. 60.3533. SI photo 56509. [87]

48. Smuggler, / By Blanco, by Irons Cadmus, by Cadmus, by American Eclipse / Winner of Champion Purse / Sept 15th 1874 / Time, 2:25, 2:23, 2:20. / Owned by Henry S. Russell, Milton, Mass.
Colored lithograph, signed in the lower right corner "E. R. Howe" and in lower left corner "Scott Leighton, del. 1874." Published by Haskell & Allen, Boston. 1874. 18 x 24¼ in. Cat. no. 60.3536. SI photo 56232. [55]

49. [Judge Fullerton Goldsmith Maid] Best Time on Record. Three Heats in 2:19¾, 2:16½, 2:16. / Goldsmith Maid and Judge Fullerton in their great trot at east saginaw, mich. [sic] July 16th 1874.
Colored lithograph. Artist, publisher, place and date of pub-

lication unknown. 18⅝ x 22¼ in. Cat. no. 60.3568. SI photo 56242. [93]

50. Goldsmith Maid. / August 12th 1874 at Rochester, N. Y. 2.14¾ / Sept. 2nd 1874 at Mystic Park 2.14 / Published by Vacuum Oil Co. Rochester, N. Y.
Colored lithograph by Donaldson Brothers, Five Points, N. Y., drawn by John Cameron. 1874. 17 x 24½ in. Cat. no. 60.3534. SI photo 56170. [96]

51. Ben Morrill, / Owned by T. B. Williams (Boston Mass.) Got by Winthrop Morrill, Dam by Old Columbus. / Won a number of Trots in 1874 and trotted at Prospect Park, Oct. 29th 1874. / Best Time 2:28 / From the Original Painting by Scott Leighton.
Colored lithograph drawn by E. R. Howe. Published by Haskell & Allen, Boston. 1875. 17½ x 25¼ in. Cat. no. 60.3538. SI photo 56280. [98]

52. Great Eastern, / As He Appeared in the Trio Races with Smuggler at Mystic Park, Boston, Oct. 16, 1876, / when the latter was distanced in first race, and beaten in the second / Time 2:21, 2:24½, 2:25.
Colored lithograph drawn by E. R. Howe. Published by Haskell & Allen, Boston. 1877. 17⅝ x 25⅛ in. Cat. no. 60.3537. SI photo 56231. [99]

53. Rarus, / The Fastest Trotting Horse in the World. / Best Time 2.13¼.
Colored lithograph. Published by F. M. Haskell & Co., Boston. 1878. 18 x 25¼ in. Cat. no. 60.3535. SI photo 56219. [100]

54. Jay Eye See. / Best Time 2.10¾ at Providence, R. I. Sept. 15th 1884. / Published by Vacuum Oil Company Rochester, N. Y.
Black-and-white photo-oleograph by Clay & Richmond, Buffalo. 1884. 15¼ x 20⅛ in. Cat. no. 60.3591. SI photo 56222. [103]

55. The Greatest Performance in Double Harness on Record —a 2:12 Gait to a Road Wagon. / Lady Palmer and Flatbush Mare, driven by their Owner, Mr. Bonner—taken out of his Stable, untrained—to a Road Wagon in Public.— / May 10, 1862.—ONE MILE in 2:26. May 13, 1862.—TWO MILES in 5:01¼—The SECOND QUARTER of the SECOND MILE in 33 SECONDS, being a 2:12 gait to a Road Wagon.
Colored lithograph by Thomas & Eno, New York. Undated. 14¼ x 19⅞ in. Cat. no. 60.3579. SI photo 56164. [106]

56. General Butler and Dexter. / Match for $2,000, two Mile heats, to Wagons, over the Fashion Course, L. I. Octr. 27th 1865. / H. Woodruff's Br. G. Dexter 1. 1. 1. D. Tallman's Bl. G. General Butler 2. 2. 2.
Colored lithograph. Artist, publisher, place and date of publication unknown. 18⅛ x 21⅛ in. Cat. no. 60.3567. SI photo 56180. [109]

57. Dexter, / The Renowned Horse Dexter, as he Appeared on Fashion Course, L. I. Driven by Hiram Woodruff.
Colored lithograph. Artist, publisher, place and date of publication unknown. 19¼ x 25⅛ in. Cat. no. 60.3588. SI photo 56203. [110]

58. Dexter, / Dexter is a brown gelding 15 hands 1 inch high foaled in 1858 sired by Rysdyk's HAMBLETONIAN / Dam Hawkins Mare by AMERICAN STAR he was raised by Jonathan Hawkins Montgomery Orange Co., N. Y. / The renowned horse Dexter as he appeared on Fashion Course L. I. driven by Hiram Woodruff / Dexter's fastest time 2:16¾ on Fashion Course June 21st 1867.
Colored lithograph. Published and printed by Thomas Kelly, New York. 1867. 8 x 12 in. Cat. no. 60.3606. SI photo 56246. [111]

59. Marsden's American Horses. / Ethan Allen. / The Property of J. E. Maynard, Esq. Time: 2.15–2.16–2.19.

Colored lithograph by C. H. Crosby, Boston; drawn by Theodore Marsden. 1868. 16 x 21⅛ in. Cat. no. 60.3565. SI photo 56158. [112]

60. Ethan Allen.
Colored lithograph. Published by Haskell & Allen, Boston. Undated. 8 x 12 in. Cat. no. 60.3603. SI photo 56272. [113]

61. Gen. Butler, Silus Rich & Bashaw Jr. / Trotting for a Purse of $2,800, or Handecaps [sic] 3 in 5 Mile Heats, at Dexter Park, Chicago, Ill. Sept. 5th 1867 / TIME 2.31¼–2.28¾–2.30¼.
Colored lithograph. Published by George Kelly, place of publication unknown. 1869. 19¼ x 25 in. Cat. no. 60.3586. SI photo 56207. [116]

62. Lady Thorne and American Girl / In Their Great Match for $2,500 Mile Heats Best 3 in 5 to Wagons. / Over the Fashion Course, L. I. July 12th 1869. / M. Roden B. M. American Girl–1121 / B. Pfifers [sic] B. M. Lady Thorne–2211 [sic] / Time, 2,28½. 2,24¾. 2,27¾. 2,24½.
Colored lithograph. Published by George Kelly, place of publication unknown. 1869. 16⅞ x 24½ in. Cat. no. 60.3589. SI photo 56515. [117]

63. Volunteer / Sired by Rysdyk's Hambletonian, Dam by Young Patriot &c. &c. / Property of Alden Goldsmith, Blooming Grove, Orange Co., N. Y.
Colored lithograph, painted by Charles S. Humphreys and lithographed by L. Geissler. Printed by Mayer & Merkel, New York. 1869. 17⅝ x 24 in. Cat. no. 60.3566. SI photo 56173. [56]

Portraits of Trotters

64. Flora Temple. / 2.24½ in harness; Union Course, L. I. Sept. 2, 1856. / (Issued with Porter's Spirit of the Times.)
Colored wood engraving, signed in lower left corner "Hitchcock A. J. Anthony Sc." Undated. 10 x 13½ in. Cat. no. 60.3620. SI photo 56245. [122]

65. Flora Temple. / The Property of Wm. McDonald Esq. Baltimore. / Photographed by Fredericks from the Original Printing by W. F. Attwood in possession of W. McDonald Esq.
Colored lithograph, after a painting by William F. Attwood, horse-portrait painter at George Murray's Stables, New York. Publisher and place of publication unknown. 1859. 17 x 19½ in. Cat. no. 60.3594. SI photo 56514. [124]

66. The Celebrated American Trotting Mare, / Flora Temple and Colt. / Now Owned by / George Welch, / Chestnut Hill, Pa.
Colored lithograph by N. Mitton, published by John Smith —both of Philadelphia. 1869. 17⅝ x 24¼ in. Cat. no. 60.3531. SI photo 56510. [126]

67. Untitled [Flora Temple and Colt].
Colored lithograph, from a painting by James Queen after E. Troye. Published by Bradley & Company, Philadelphia. 1869. 17⅞ x 23⅞ in. Cat. no. 60.3545. SI photo 56220. [127]

68. Untitled [Flora Temple and Colt].
Colored lithograph. Signature in lower right corner illegible. Artist, publisher, place and date of publication unknown. 14⅞ x 20⅜ in. Cat. no. 60.3541. SI photo 56214.

69. Trotting Gallery / From a picture by W. F. Attwood, 1860. / Published by Brewster & Co., Carriage Makers. / Nos 372 & 374 Broome, Cor. of Mott Streets,–New York. / First Class Road and Trotting Wagons a Specialty.
Colored lithograph by Sarony, Major & Knapp, New York. 1860. 16½ x 27½ in. Cat. no. 60.3551. SI photo 56182. [129]

70. Hambletonian. / The property of Wm. M. Rysdyk of Chester, Orange County, New York. / Was sired by Old Abdallah, he by Mambrino, and he by imported Messenger. His dam was the Charles Kent mare by imported Bellfounder; grand dam, old One Eye by old Hambletonian, and / he by imported Messenger; and his dam also by imported Messenger, and the dam of Old One Eye was by imported Messenger.
Colored lithograph, from a painting by Theodore Marsden. Published by Henry C. Eno, New York, and drawn on stone by Henry A. Thomas. 1866. 19 x 25 in. Cat. no. 60.3528. SI photo 56511. [131]

71. Rysdyk's Hambletonian. / Was sired by old Abdallah, he by Mambrino, and he by imported Messenger. His dam was the Charles Kent mare by imported Bellfounder; . . .
Colored lithograph, lithographed in colors by Henry C. Eno after a painting by James H. Wright, drawn on stone by L. Geissler, and published by John J. Olone, all of New York. 1866. 19 x 25⅛ in. Cat. no. 60.3544. SI photo 56218. [57]

72. Volunteer. / Sired by Rysdyk's Hambletonian, Dam by Young Patriot &c. &c. / Property of Alden Goldsmith, Blooming Grove Orange Co. N. Y.
Colored lithograph, after a painting by Charles S. Humphreys; signed in lower left corner "H. Thomas, 64." Printed and published by Henry C. Eno, New York. 1864. 13¾ x 17¼ in. Cat. no. 60.3574. SI photo 56292. [132]

73. Untitled [Mambrino Champion].
Colored lithograph, signed in lower right corner "J. Cameron 1867." Publisher, place and date of publication unknown. 18⅝ x 25 in. Cat. no. 60.3543. SI photo 56217. [135]

74. Untitled.
Black-and-white lithograph from life by A. C. Webb, Nashville. Undated. 19 x 24½ in. Cat. no. 60.3570. SI photo 56178. [136]

75. Rarus. / Best Time on Record 2.13¼ Buffalo, N. Y. Aug. 3rd 1878. / Published by Vacuum Oil Company Rochester, N. Y.
Black-and-white engraving, signed in lower right corner "Kittridge, Del." Engraved and printed by Homer Lee & Co., New York. 1878. 15¼ x 20½ in. Cat. no. 60.3592. SI photo 56224. [137]

76. St. Julien—2.12¾ Oakland, Cal. Oct. 25, 1879.
Colored lithograph by E. Bosqui & Company, San Francisco; signed in lower right corner "W. Harring." Published by the San Francisco Bulletin Company. 1880. 21¼ x 29¼ in. Cat. no. 60.3542. SI photo 56215. [139]

77. Wedgewood 692. / By Belmont—Woodbine, / Record 2.19.
Black-and-white lithograph by Mayer, Merkel & Ottman, New York, signed in the lower left corner "A. J. Schultz 3–85." 1885. 17 x 23⅞ in. Cat. no. 60.3546. SI photo 56512. [140]

78. Cresceus / 1.59¾.
Colored lithograph. Published by the Frontier Lithograph Co. Buffalo. 1903. 8 x 11 in. Cat. no. 60.3621. SI photo 56244. [142]

Handbills and Broadsides

79. Blooded Stock. / For Sale by Auction, / Under the Direction of the Proprietors of the "New York Tattersalls," / At Mr. John R. Snedicor's / Near the Union Course, Long Island, / On Friday, June 2, 1837, at 10 o'clock, A.M.
Broadside, engraved and signed by E. Forbes, wood engraver. Printed by Jared W. Bell, New York. June 1, 1837. 11½ x 7½ in. Cat. no. 60.3600. SI photo 56227. [150]

80. St. Patrick.
Wood-engraved broadside, signed "Anderson," Rotterdam,

[N. Y.]. May 12, 1838. 13¾ x 9½ in. Cat. no. 60.3598. SI photo 56228.   [144]

81. Vendue.
Wood-block engraving. Printed at the Reflector office [Rotterdam, N. Y.]. November 13, 1838. 8⅝ x 7 in. Cat. no. 60.3599. SI photo 56226.   [149]

82. The Horse / Trustee, / The Sire of Fashion, Revenue, &c. &c. / Also, Is the Sire of the Celebrated / Trotting Horse Trustee

Wood-engraved broadside. Printed by Jared W. Bell, New York. February, 1849. 31½ x 17 in. Cat. no. 60.3597. SI photo 56516.   [151]

83. Hartford Races / Charter Oak Park / August 27, 28, 29, 30, 1889.
(Illuminated race poster by Currier and Ives, New York, with vignette title "A Good Race, Well Won.") Colored lithograph, signed in lower right corner "Thos. Worth." Undated. 18 x 26¾ in. (vignette); 41½ x 29½ in. (overall). Cat. no. 60.3229. SI photo 56185.   [58]

The information listed below includes the names, places, and title designations that actually appear on the prints themselves. (To aid in identification, Smithsonian catalog numbers and other particulars are sometimes given.) General information—career working dates, other prints published, etc.—may be found in Peters, *America on Stone*, and in such standard works as Groce and Wallace, Fielding, and Stokes.

Anderson (engraver)
St. Patrick

Hitchcock A. J. Anthony (engraver)
Flora Temple

William F. Attwood
Flora Temple

J. Beard
Fast Horses, of N. Y.

J. W. Bell, 17 Ann Street, New York
Blooded Stock

Jared W. Bell, 178 Fulton Street, New York
Trustee

E. Bosqui & Company, San Francisco
St. Julien

Bradley & Company, 66 North Fourth Street, Philadelphia
Untitled [Flora Temple and Colt]

Brewster & Co., Broome Street, New York
Road Scenes, No. 1. "The Shed"

J. H. Bufford, 313 Washington Street, Boston

J. H. Bufford & Sons, Boston
Winter. Going to a Christmas Party
Sherman Black Hawk
The Famous Roan Horse Capt. McGowan

J. Cameron (also J. N. C.)
Untitled (sleigh race)
Goldsmith Maid
Untitled [Mambrino Champion]

Charles Brothers, New York
Winter in the Country

Childs & Inman, Philadelphia
Columbus

Robert A. Clarke
Lady Suffolk (60.3548)
Lady Suffolk (60.3550)
Celebrated American Trotting Horses

E. Clarkson, Philadelphia
Andrew Jackson Jr.

Clay & Richmond, Buffalo
Jay Eye See (photo-oleograph)

C. H. Crosby, Boston
Ethan Allen

Currier & Ives, 115 Nassau Street, New York
Hartford Races

Donaldson Brothers, Five Points, N. Y.
Goldsmith Maid

L. G. Eaton
Fearnaught Stallions (60.3555)

John W. Ehninger
"Taking the Reins"

Samuel Emerson, Riverside Riding Park, Brighton, Mass.
The Famous Roan Horse Capt. McGowan

George Endicott, New York
Columbus and Sally Miller

Endicott & Co., 59 Beekman Street, New York
Road Scenes, No. 1. "The Shed"

Henry C. Eno, 37 Park Row, New York
Hambletonian
Rysdyk's Hambletonian
Volunteer (60.3574)

E. Forbes (engraver)
Blooded Stock

Frontier Lithograph Co., Buffalo
Cresceus

F. Fudes(?)
Winter Pleasure in the Country

L. Geissler
Volunteer (60.3566)
Rysdyk's Hambletonian

W. Harring
St. Julien

Charles Hart, New York
Winter in the Country

G. G. Hartwell
Untitled (60.3617)

Haskell & Allen, 61 Hanover Street, 14 Hanover Street, Boston
Leaving Brighton Hotel for the Mill-Dam. Summer
Trotting Cracks on the Brighton Road. (Scene, Mile Ground.)
Leaving Brighton Hotel for the Mill-Dam. Winter
Winter
Fearnaught Stallions (60.3555)
Fearnaught Stallions (60.3605)
Untitled (60.3540)
Dexter, Ethan Allen and Mate (60.3530)
Smuggler
Ben Morrill
Great Eastern
Ethan Allen

F. M. Haskell & Co., 61 Hanover Street, Boston
Rarus

Richard S. Hillman
Columbus (60.3602)
Whalebone

A. Hoen & Co., Baltimore
Andrew Jackson Jr.

E. R. Howe
Leaving Brighton Hotel for the Mill-Dam. Summer
Untitled (60.3539)
Smuggler
Ben Morrill
Great Eastern

Hughes & Johnson, Chicago
A Merry Christmas. A Happy New-Year

Charles S. Humphreys
Sherman Black Hawk
Volunteer (60.3566)
Volunteer (60.3574)

Imbert, New York
To Mr. John Roulstone of the New York Riding School

E. Jones & G. W. Newman, 128 Fulton Street, Sun Building, New York
Wake up there! What'r ye' 'bout?

George Kelly, Philadelphia

Gen. Butler, Silus Rich & Bashaw Jr.
Lady Thorne and American Girl

J. Kelly & Sons, Philadelphia and New York
Winter Scene in the Country

Thomas Kelly, 17 Barclay Street, 35 Bowery, New York
Watering Place on the Road
Going to the Trot
Trotting Cracks on the Road. Scene Harlem Lane
Fast Horses, of N. Y.
A Home in the Country
Dexter, Ethan Allen and Mate (60.3533)
Dexter

Kennedy & Lucas, Philadelphia
Whalebone

Kimmel & Forster, New York
Winter Pleasure in the Country

J. D. M. Kisson, Perrysville, Ohio
Prince Imperial

Kitteridge
Rarus

W. Kurtz, New York
Watering Place on the Road

Homer Lee & Co., New York
Rarus

Scott Leighton
Smuggler

George W. Lewis, 122 Fulton Street, New York
Lady Suffolk (60.3550)

[164]

Lewis & Brown, 37 John Street, New York
Lady Suffolk (60.3548)

Theodore Marsden
Ethan Allen
Hambletonian

Mayer & Merkel, 141 Fulton Street, New York
Volunteer (60.3566)

Mayer, Merkel & Ottman, New York
Wedgewood 692

N. Mitton, Philadelphia
The Celebrated American Trotting Mare, Flora Temple and Colt

J. A. Oertel
Road Scenes, No. 1. "The Shed"

John J. Olone, 845 Broadway, New York
Rysdyk's Hambletonian

F. & S. Palmer, 43 Ann Street, New York
No. 1! and *northin* else
Take ca-are what ar-ye 'bout
Two of the B'hoys
Heigh---gh! Wake up there, what are ye at?

H. Pharazyn, Philadelphia
Trotting Cracks of Philadelphia Returning from the Race at Point Breeze Park

James Queen
Untitled [Flora Temple and Colt]
Point Breeze Park

W. H. Rease, 97 Chestnut Street, Philadelphia
Celebrated American Trotting Horses

Reflector Office, 116 State Street, Rotterdam, N. Y.
Vendue

Wm. C. Robertson, 59 Cedar Street, New York
Winter Scene in the Country
Dexter, Ethan Allen and Mate

H. R. Robinson, 142 Nassau Street, New York
Horse at Liberty

San Francisco Bulletin Company
St. Julien

Sarony, Major & Knapp, 449 Broadway, New York
Trotting Gallery

A. J. Schultz
Wedgewood 692

Thomas Sinclair, Philadelphia
Point Breeze Park

John Smith, 710 Sansom Street, Philadelphia
The Celebrated American Trotting Mare, Flora Temple and Colt

Tappan & Bradford, Boston
Untitled (60.3617)

Henry A. Thomas
  Hambletonian
  Volunteer (60.3574)

Thomas & Eno, 37 Park Row, New York
  The Greatest Performance in Double Harness on
  Record
  Hambletonian
  Volunteer (60.3574)

Wagner & McGuigan, Philadelphia
  Celebrated American Trotting Horses

M. J. Warner
  Deacon Jones' One Hoss Shay. No. 1
  Deacon Jones' One Hoss Shay. No. 2

A. C. Webb, Nashville
  Untitled (60.3570)

Thomas Worth
  Hartford Races

James H. Wright
  Rysdyk's Hambletonian

American Agriculturist. New York, 1842+.

American Turf and Sporting Magazine. New York, 1829–1844.

Bradburn, John. *Breeding and Developing the Trotter.* Boston, 1906.

Burgess, James W. *A Practical Treatise on Coach-Building Historical and Descriptive.* London, 1881.

Chance, Elbert. Fast Horses and Sporting Blood, *Delaware History,* vol. 9 (October 1964).

Chester, Walter T., compil. *Chester's Complete Trotting and Pacing Record, Containing Summaries of all Races Trotted or Paced in the United States or Canada from the Earliest to the Close of 1883.* New York, 1884.

Cole, Arthur C. Our Sporting Grandfathers. *The Atlantic Monthly* (July 1932).

Dulles, Foster Rhea. *America Learns to Play.* New York and London, 1940.

Duncan, William Cary. *Golden Hoofs, the True Story of an Amazing Mare* [Goldsmith Maid]. Philadelphia and New York, 1937.

Durant, John, and Bettmann, Otto. *Pictorial History of American Sports.* New York, 1952.

Eighty Years' Progress of the United States. Hartford, 1867.

Feek, A. J. *Every Man His Own Trainer, or How to Develop, Condition and Train a Trotter or Pacer.* Syracuse, 1889.

Fielding, Mantle. *Dictionary of American Painters, Sculptors, and Engravers.* Philadelphia, 1926.

Frank Leslie's Illustrated Newspaper. New York, 1855–1922.

Geer, Ed. *Ed Geer's Experience with Trotters and Pacers.* Buffalo, 1901.

Groce, George C., and Wallace, David H. *The New-York Historical Society's Dictionary of Artists in America 1564–1860.* New Haven, 1957.

Herbert, Henry William [Frank Forester]. *Frank Forester's Horse and Horsemanship of the United States and British Provinces of North America.* 2 vols. New York, 1871. (First edition New York, 1857.)

Howard, Robert W. *The Horse in America.* New York, 1965.

Huth, F. H. *Works on Horses and Equitation: A Bibliographical Record of Hippology.* London, 1887.

Krout, John Allen. *The Annals of American Sport.* New Haven, 1929.

Linsley, D. C. *Morgan Horses.* New York, 1857.

McCartney, John. *The Story of a Great Horse. Cresceus, 2:02¼.* Indianapolis, 1902.

McClure, Robert, ed. *Every Horse Owners' Cyclopedia.* Philadelphia, 1872.

Murrell, William. *A History of American Graphic Humor.* 2 vols. New York, 1933–1938.

Paxon, F. The Rise of Sport. *Mississippi Valley Historical Review,* vol. 4 (September 1917).

Peters, Harry T. *America on Stone; the Other Printmakers to the American People.* Garden City, N. Y., 1931.

————. *Currier & Ives, Printmakers to the American People.* 2 vols. Garden City, N. Y., 1929–1931.

Sanders, Millard. *The Two-Minute Horse. A History of the Six Two-Minute Trotters and the Fourteen Two-Minute Pacers to the Close of the Year 1921.* Cleveland, 1922.

Stillman, J. D. B. *The Horse in Motion, as Shown by Instantaneous Photography* [Muybridge]. Boston, 1882.

Wallace, John H. *The Horse of America.* New York, 1897.

————. *Wallace's American Stud-Book.* New York, 1867.

Welsh, Peter C. Productive in Their Pleasures. *The Smithsonian Journal of History*, vol. 1 (Summer 1966), pp. 1–8.

————. The Trotter. *American Heritage*, vol. 18 (December 1966), pp. 30–49.

———— (with Anthony Garvan). *The Victorian American*. Washington, D.C., 1961.

Westcott, Edward Noyes. *David Harum: A Story of American Life*. New York, 1898.

Woodruff, Hiram. *The Trotting Horse of America, How to Train and Drive Him. With Reminiscences of the Trotting Turf*. New York, 1868.

(Names of horses appear in italics.)

Abdallah, 130
Albany cutter, 36
American Art Union, 72, 133
American Girl, 95
Attwood, William F., 123, 125, 128

Babylon, N.Y., 67
Baltimore, Md., 125
Bashaw Jr., 114, 115, 119
Bay George, 18
Bay Mary, 18
Beacon Course (Camden, N.J.), 45, 64
Beacon Course (Hoboken, N.J.), 67, 68
Bell, Jared W., 145, 147
Bellfounder, 130
Belmont, 138
Ben Morrill, 97
Bithers, Ned, 104
Black Hawk, 12, 88, 123
Black Maggie, 18
Black Maria, 128
Bonner, Robert, 18, 73, 102, 105, 138
Booth, Henry, 147
Boston, 1, 14, 23, 36, 53, 67, 97
Bowen, J. J., 82, 84, 97
Brady, Matthew, 125
Bravo, 145
Brewster & Co. (New York), 8, 14, 128
Bridgeport, Conn., 128
Brown, George S., 125
Browne, Junius Henri, 17
Brunette, 130
Bruno, 130
Bryant, David, 68, 72
Buffalo, N.Y., 102
Buggy, 12, 16, 17, 49
Burgess, James W., 12
Business wagon, 8

California, 1, 48
Cambridge Course (Massachusetts), 64
Cambridge, Mass., 45, 46
Campbell, D. D., 146
Canada, 91, 97
Captain McGowan, 82, 84
Carriage, 49, 53, 91, 128
Centreville Course (Massachusetts), 64
Chaise, 7, 49
Charlotte F., 90
Charter Oak Park (Hartford, Conn.), 50, 51, 148
Chicago, 26, 45
Civil War, 2
Clarke, Robert A., 68, 72
Cleveland, Ohio, 45
Coach, 8, 128
Columbus, 46, 61, 64, 72, 114
Columbus, Ohio, 141
Comet, 46, 64
Concklin, R. B., 102
Conklin, Albert, 67, 68, 72
Connecticut, 1, 10, 48
Cresceus, 44, 45, 50, 141

Dewey, Foster, 18
Dexter, 18, 44, 48, 53, 54, 73, 75, 84, 85, 88, 89, 90, 102, 107, 108, 114, 115, 123
Dexter Park (Chicago), 114
Dey of Algiers, 10
M. H. de Young Museum, 4
Dictator, 134
Doble, Budd, 52, 54, 59, 60, 75, 85, 90, 94, 95, 97
Driving Park (Buffalo, N.Y.), 92
Driving Park (Cleveland, Ohio), 92
Driving Park (East Saginaw, Mich.), 92, 94
Driving Park (Rochester, N.Y.), 95
Duroc, 11, 145
Dutchman, 52, 60

Eastman, Timothy, 18
East Saginaw, Mich., 92
Eclipse, 10, 145
Edwin Forest, 67
Elderken, John, 18
Emerson, Samuel, 82
England, 7
Ethan Allen, 44, 84, 85, 88, 89, 90, 108, 114, 115, 123, 128

Fairs:
    Goshen Horse Fair, 134
    United States Agricultural Fair (West Philadelphia), 78, 81
Fanny Allen, 18
Fanny Pullen, 147
Fashion Course (Long Island), 84, 90, 105, 108, 115, 118
Fearnaught, 92
Feek, A. J., 101
Flatbush Mare, 105, 107
Flora Temple, 44, 48, 68, 72, 73, 94, 104, 121, 123, 125, 128
Forbes E., 145
Forester, Frank (Henry William Herbert), 7, 8, 9, 47, 64, 68, 72, 85, 107, 114, 123, 130, 133 146
Foster, Charles, 85, 123
Fredricks, Charles D., 125
French Canada, 10

Geers, Ed, 77
General Birney, 18
General Butler, 107, 108, 114, 115, 118, 119
George M. Patchen, 128
George Wilkes, 130, 134
Gig, 49, 53
Gillander, A. J., 18
Gold Rush era, 1
Goldsmith, Alden, 119

Goldsmith Maid, 18, 44, 48, 53, 54, 92, 94, 95, 97, 101, 102, 115, 119
Grand Bashaw, 115
Grand Circuit, 49, 50, 91, 97, 105, 138
Grant, General Ulysses S., 18, 138
Great Eastern, 92, 97, 101

Haliburton, Thomas Chandler, 37
Hall of Fame of the Trotter (Goshen, N.Y.), 138
Hambletonian, 11, 12, 73, 77, 88, 119, 128, 130, 133, 134, 138
Hampdon Park (Springfield, Mass.), 92
Harlem Lane (New York), 14, 49
Harry D., 18
Hartford, Conn., 45, 50, 51
Henry, 10
Herbert, Henry William. *See* Frank Forester
Hickok, Orrin, 138
Highland Maid, 72, 73
Hillman, Richard, 64, 77
Holmes, Oliver Wendell, 37, 51, 52, 54, 59
Horses:
COLORS OF, 12, 53
BREEDS: Abdallah, 94, 102
Arabian, 10
Danish, 10
English racer, 10
Flemish, 10
Hambletonian, 133, 138
Mambrino, 134
Messenger, 130, 138
Morgan, 11, 78
Norman, 10;
TYPES: American roadster, 9, 10, 11
American trotter, 7, 9, 11, 17, 23, 26, 37, 42, 43, 47, 51, 60, 61, 72, 75, 130, 143, 145, 148, 149
buggy, 16
draft, 10, 11

driving, 10, 11
farm, 10, 11
galloper, 11
gelding, 61, 73, 77, 82, 97, 104, 138
hunter, 143
runner, 11, 143
saddle, 11
studs, 11, 121, 130, 133, 134, 138, 145, 146, 147
Humphreys, Charles S., 78, 81, 133, 134
"Hunting Park Association for the Improvement of Trotting Horses" (Philadelphia), 44
Hunting Park Course (Philadelphia), 64, 81

Imported Messenger, 10, 53, 64, 77, 88, 130, 145
Ironsides, 18

Jack Rossiter, 72
Jay Eye See, 50, 102, 104, 138
Joe Parker Pony, 18
Jones Richard, 115
Judge Fullerton, 92, 94, 95
Justin Morgan, 10, 12, 53, 88

Kelly, George, 114, 118, 119
Kent, Charles, 130
Kentucky, 82, 118
Kinney Bros., 68

Lady Fulton, 84
Lady Lightfoot, 18
Lady Palmer, 105
Lady Suffolk ("The Old Gray Mare"), 44, 46, 53, 54, 64, 68, 72, 94, 123, 128
Lawrence, J. E., 82
Leavenworth, Kans., 92
Leighton, Scott, 138
Lexington, Ky., 134

Linsley, D. C., 11, 78
Lithograph collections: Peters California on Stone Collection, 4; Peters Currier & Ives Collection, 4; Peters America on Stone Collection, 4, 14, 18, 44, 45, 61, 64, 68, 72, 73, 75, 77, 97, 102, 104, 105, 108, 114, 119, 120, 121, 125, 128, 133, 134, 138, 141, 145, 148
Lithographers and publishers:
E. Bosqui & Co., 50, 138
Bradley & Co., 125
Britton (New York), 1
Bufford, John, 1, 23, 36, 47, 78
Bufford & Sons, 82
Cameron, J., 36, 108, 134
Charles Brothers, 26
Clay & Richmond, 50
C. H. Crosby (Boston), 108
Currier & Ives, 1, 2, 3, 9, 17, 36, 41, 94, 95, 97, 104, 107, 134, 148
L. W. Cushing & Sons (Waltham, Mass.), 89
Donaldson Brothers (Five Points, N.Y.), 95
Duval, Peter, 1
P. S. Duvall & Co., 81
Endicott, George, 61
Endicotts (New York), 1, 14
Fiske, J. W., 89
Frontier Lithograph Co., 50, 141
Hart, Charles, 26
Haskell & Allen (Boston), 1, 18, 23, 26, 36, 48, 84, 85, 89, 90, 91, 92, 97, 101, 114, 138
F. M. Haskell & Co. (Boston), 101, 108
A. Hoen & Co. (Baltimore), 14
Hughes & Johnson, 26
Jackson, W. G., 107
Jones & Newman, 36
Kelloggs (New York), 1
Kelly, John, 26

Kelly, Thomas, 18, 26, 89, 108
Kennedy & Lucas (Philadelphia), 77
Kimmel & Forster, 26
Lewis, George W., 68
Lewis & Brown, 64, 67, 68
Mayer & Merkel (New York), 118
Mayer, Merkle & Ottman, 138
Olone, John J., 130
Otis, Bass, 1
Rease, W. H., 44, 72
Rey (San Francisco), 1
Robinson, Henry, 1
San Francisco Bulletin Co., 138
Sarony, Major, and Knapp (New York),
   1, 14, 128
Senefelder, Alois, 1
Sinclair, Thomas, 1, 81
Smith, John, 125
Thomas & Eno, 105, 130, 133
Wagner & McGuigan (Philadelphia),
   44
Warner, M. J., 37
Wilkes, George, 121, 123
London, 125
Long Island Trotting Club, 44

Mac, 72, 73
Macdonald, William, 125
Mace, Dan, 90
Mack, 18
Major Winfield, 130
Mambrino, 64
Mambrino Champion, 134
Mambrino Chief, 12, 118, 134
Mambrino Pilot, 92
Marquis of Donegal, 146
Marsden, Theodore, 107, 108, 114, 128,
   130
Marvin, Charles, 91
Massachusetts, 10, 48
Maud S, 45, 51, 102

Maynard, J. E., 114
McCartney, John, 141
Michigan, 48, 94
Missouri, 48
Morris County Agricultural Soicety, 90
Morristown, N.J., 89
Morven, N.J., 147
Moscow, 18
Mountain Boy, 18
Museum of the City of New York, 4
Mystic Park (Boston), 45, 90, 91, 95, 97,
   101

Napoleon, 18
National Academy (New York), 123, 133
Nevins, David, Jr., 36
New Hampshire, 48
New Haven, Conn., 128
New Jersey, 11
New Orleans, 1, 67
Newport, R. I., 14, 16
New York, 7, 10, 11, 48, 82, 97, 145
New York City, 9, 17, 23, 53, 72, 89, 125,
   128
New York Trotting Club, 44
Niagara Falls, 10

Oakland, Calif., 45
Ohio, 11, 92
Old Blue, 52
Old Hiram, 54, 59
Omnibus, 49
Oneida Chief, 67
Orange County, N.Y., 73, 133

Paris, 125
Pennsylvania, 11
Pennsylvania Academy, 72
Periodicals
   American Agriculturist, 47, 73, 77
   American Farmer, 43

American Turf Register, 43
Atlantic, 52
Boston Daily Globe, 48, 49
Cambridge Chronicle, 46
Daily Chronicle (Philadelphia), 45
Daily News (Philadelphia), 78
Frank Leslie's Illustrated Newspaper, 43
Hartford Courant, 50, 51, 148
Harvard Advocate, 51
Horse World, 141
National Gazette, 45, 64
New York Daily Tribune, 17, 46, 90
New York Ledger, 18, 105
New York Times, 84, 85
Spirit of the Times, 67, 121
Sporting Magazine, 43
Sporting Times, 82
Wilkes' Spirit of the Times, 123
Peters, Harry T., 1, 3, 4, 7, 64, 94, 97,
   107, 108, 121, 145. See also Lithograph
   collections
Pfeiffer (Pfifer), Dan, 52, 54, 60, 118
Philadelphia, 14, 49, 53, 72, 81, 115
Point Breeze Park (Philadelphia), 14, 45,
   50, 75, 81
Poor Richard, 3
Porter, William T., 67, 121, 123
Post Boy, 10
Powelton Grounds (West Philadelphia),
   78, 81
Princess, 128
Publishers. See Lithographers and pub-
   lishers

Queen, James, 81, 82, 125

Rarus, 44, 45, 92, 95, 101, 102, 138
Red Cloud, 18
Rhode Island, 48
Richmond, 146
Riverside Riding Park (Brighton, Mass.),
   82

Road Wagon, 9, 108
Rochester, N.Y., 45, 95, 102
Rockaway, 8
W. D. Rogers & Co. (Philadelphia), 8
Ross, Marjorie D., 36
Rotterdam, N.Y., 146
Russell, Colonel H. S., 48, 92
Rysdyk, William, 130, 133

St. Julien, 44, 45, 50, 102, 119, 138
St. Patrick, 146
Sally Miller, 46, 61, 64, 72
San Francisco, 45
San Francisco Historical Society, 4
Screwdriver, 45
Shell-shaped sleigh, 26
Sherman Black Hawk, 47, 78, 81
Silas Rich, 114
Sir Charles, 10
Sir Walter, 10
Smithsonian Institution, 4
Smuggler, 48, 90, 91, 92, 97, 101
Splan, John, 101, 102
Springfield, Ill., 64
Stage coach, 8
Stillman, J. D. B., 121
Stockton, Robert, 147
Sulky, 7, 12, 49, 61, 68, 75, 77, 105, 128

Sunbeam, 18
Sun Flower, 18

Tacony, 44, 68, 72, 73
Talma, 145
Tandem rig, 125
Tarrytown, N.Y., 102
Tattersalls (England), 145
Tennessee, 134
Thomas, Henry A., 128, 133, 134
Tocqueville, Alexis de, 148, 149
Top buggy, 8
Tough, W. E., 92
Towle, George Makepeace, 17, 23, 26, 36
Trollope, Anthony, 14, 16
Trollope, Frances, 23
Trotting wagon, 8
Troye, E., 125, 128
Trustee, 84, 147, 148

Union Course (Long Island), 64, 121, 123

Vacuum Oil Co., 138
Vanderbilt, William, 18, 95, 105, 107
Vessey, John Henry, 16, 17
Victoria, 18
Victorian America, 43, 147
Victorian Americans, 119

Victorian attitudes, 2, 3
Victorian era, 4, 51
Victorian life, 2
Victor Patchen, 18
Virginia, 145
Volunteer, 119, 130, 133, 134, 138

Wagon, 7, 49, 53, 61, 68, 75, 105, 107, 108, 114, 128, 146, 148
Wainwright, Nicholas B., 81, 82
Wallace, John, 82, 85, 88
Watson, Elkanah, 47
Webb, A. C., 134
Wedgewood 692, 138, 141
Welch, George, 125
Westcott, Edward Noyes, 37
Whalebone, 77, 78, 114
Whelan, Peter, 61
Winsor, Justin, 23
Woodruff, Hiram, 23, 44, 46, 52, 60, 61, 68, 72, 73, 75, 77, 81, 85, 107, 108, 123, 141, 147
Wright, James, 130, 133

Yankee, 44
Young Trafalgar, 18

Zachary Taylor, 72

This book was set in Caledonia and Bodoni types by the Monotype Composition Company of Baltimore, Maryland, and reproduced on Mohawk Superfine paper by the Vinmar Lithographing Company of Baltimore, Maryland